Supporting Multilingual Learners in the Early Years

Are children who are exposed to more than one language from birth at an advantage or a disadvantage when starting school?

Supporting Multilingual Learners in the Early Years examines the theoretical, ideological and practical issues involved in the education of children speaking two or more languages coming to settings which are predominantly monolingual. The book examines current research and thinking about the advantages and disadvantages of being multilingual and tackles complex topics such as:

- what being multilingual implies in terms of prior learning and why this matters in education;
- the importance of respect for diversity and encouraging children to be proud of their language and culture;
- practical ways to help young children acquire English;
- ways of working with parents who themselves have little or no English;
- the differences and difficulties involved in a child learning an additional language so early on in their lives;
- strategies for exploring the learning of multilingual learners and a review of the resources and activities that could help.

Sandra Smidt views multilingualism as a cognitive advantage and shows how early years practitioners can use interactive styles of learning to focus on the benefit that the many cultures and languages in the classroom can bring to children's learning and development.

Written in a highly accessible tone, this book offers practitioners a mix of practical case studies and examples in which theory is embedded and its importance explained. Students of early childhood education will also appreciate the author's carefully structured approach to the topic, as she includes summary boxes, glossaries and points for reflection in each chapter.

CORNWALL COLLEGE
LEARNING CENTRE

Sandra Smidt was formerly Principal Lecturer in Early Childhood Education at the University of East London. She is now an educational consultant, working with the University of East London. Sandra's other books available from Routledge are *A Guide to Early Years Practice* (Third Edition); *The Developing Child in the Twenty-first Century*; and *Observing, Assessing and Planning for Children in the Early Years: A Reader*.

The Nursery World/Routledge Essential Guides for Early Years Practitioners

Books in this series, specially commissioned and written in conjunction with *Nursery World* magazine, address key issues for early years practitioners working in today's nursery and school environments. Each title is packed full of practical activities, support, advice and guidance, all of which is in line with current government early years policy. The authors use their experience and expertise to write accessibly and informatively, emphasising through the use of case studies the practical aspects of the subject, whilst retaining strong theoretical underpinnings throughout.

These titles will encourage the practitioner and student alike to gain greater confidence and authority in their day-to-day work, offering many illustrative examples of good practice, suggestions for further reading and many invaluable resources. For a handy, clear and inspirational guide to understanding the important and practical issues, the early years practitioner or student need look no further than this series.

Titles in the series

Circle Time for Young Children
Jenny Mosley

Developing Positive Behaviour in the Early Years
Sue Roffey

**Identifying Additional Learning Needs in the Early Years:
Listening to the children**
Christine MacIntyre

**Understanding Children's Development in the Early Years:
Questions practitioners frequently ask**
Christine MacIntyre

Observing, Assessing and Planning for Children in the Early Years
Sandra Smidt

**Drama 3–5: A practical guide to teaching drama to children
in the foundation stage**
Debbie Chalmers

Music 3–5 (forthcoming)
Susan Young

Encouraging Creative Play and Learning in the Early Years (forthcoming)
Diane Rich

Learning and Playing Outdoors (forthcoming)
Jan White

Thinking and Learning about Maths in the Early Years (forthcoming)
Linda Pound

Essential Nursery Management (forthcoming)
Susan Hay

Supporting Multilingual Learners in the Early Years

Many languages – many children

Sandra Smidt

Routledge
Taylor & Francis Group

LONDON AND NEW YORK

First published 2008
by Routledge
2 Park Square, Milton Park, Abingdon, Oxon, OX14 4RN

Simultaneously published in the USA and Canada
by Routledge
270 Madison Avenue, New York, NY 10016

Routledge is an imprint of the Taylor & Francis Group, an informa business

© 2008 Sandra Smidt

Typeset in Perpetua and Bell Gothic by BC Typesetting Ltd, Bristol
Printed and bound in Great Britain by
TJ International Ltd, Padstow, Cornwall

British Library Cataloguing in Publication Data
A catalogue record for this book is available from the British Library

Library of Congress Cataloging in Publication Data
A catalog record for this book has been requested

ISBN 13: 978–0–415–43800–1 (hbk)
ISBN 13: 978–0–415–43801–8 (pbk)
ISBN 13: 978–0–203–93858–4 (ebk)

ISBN 10: 0–415–43800–4 (hbk)
ISBN 10: 0–415–43801–2 (pbk)
ISBN 10: 0–203–93858–5 (ebk)

Contents

Illustrations

Note

The small line drawings in this book were done by Hannah Gardiner, age 10.

In this book we use the symbol ![lightbulb symbol] to signify things that have implications for those working with bilingual or multilingual children.

Chapter 1

Understanding multilingualism

In this chapter you will start to think about multilingualism in terms of whether it is a problem or an advantage in terms of learning and development.

You will read something about some of the misconceptions and myths and prejudices that have grown up around multiculturalism.

You will consider how attitudes to multiculturalism relate to changing times and factors like immigration, economic stability and prejudice.

You will take a brief tour of how policies around multiculturalism and education have developed and changed in the UK.

You will read some case studies concerning the policies developed by some schools, settings and nurseries.

MULTILINGUALISM: AN INTRODUCTION

Did you know that, throughout the world, multilingualism is the norm and not the exception? In South Africa, for example, there are 11 official languages and it is taken for granted that almost everyone will speak two or more languages. In Nigeria there are over 500 languages spoken and in India there are said to be more than 1,600 languages. Yet in the UK, despite the fact that ours is a multicultural society where more than 300 different languages are spoken in London alone, we still tend to regard those who speak English as an additional language as being special at best and odd at worst.

Initially through British colonialisation and later through the development of technology English has become a global language. In many countries throughout the world English is offered as a second or subsequent language and it is largely considered as *the* language of business, of finance and of the internet. Children growing up in South Africa and in India and in China are expected to become fluent in English if they want to succeed. In this country we continue to be largely monolingual English speakers, expecting the rest of the world to understand our language and not doing much to develop our abilities to speak, read and write other languages.

We do tend to regard this country as an English-speaking country and it is, of course, true that children will need to be fluent speakers, readers and writers of English in order to succeed in the educational system. But the Englishness of this country has had a long history which has involved moving from 'Old English' to the language which predominates today. Reid (1993) tells us that French was the language of the ruling classes, of the intelligentsia and of the rich for three or four centuries after the Norman Conquest and English was the language of the uneducated and the unschooled. So English was seen as an inferior language. That is fascinating when one examines some of the things that are said about languages today. Here are some of these for you to consider:

1   Sumiyo's teacher tells her mother: 'Try and ensure that you only speak English at home.'
2   A booklet for parents of children in a day nursery suggests: 'Use English all the time because if your child is bilingual he will be at a disadvantage.'
3   At a parents' evening the headteacher organises a meeting for the parents of children who have English as an additional language and tells them that the best way for their children to learn English is in small, separate groups, out of the classroom.
4   Thomas has just started secondary school and his father wanted to know what choice of languages there was in the school and said he would like Thomas to be able to learn Turkish. The head of languages told him that they offered German, Spanish and French and would be introducing Mandarin, but Turkish would be 'of little use'.
5   A university lecturer visiting a teaching student in a multilingual primary classroom asked the teacher how

multilingual children were supported in learning English and was told that the main object was for children to learn a lot of words, particularly names of objects.

These comments reveal prejudices, misconceptions and myths not only associated with what it means to know more than one language but also about how children who do should be taught. Let us look at each in turn.

1   Sumiyo speaks Japanese at home with her parents and siblings and with her extended family. She speaks Japanese when the family returns to Tokyo each summer. She speaks English at her nursery. The advice for her mother to speak to her in English threatens to risk that she will lose her first language and, as you will see as you read on, identity is very closely tied up with home language or languages. More than that, for Sumiyo Japanese is the language with which she is most familiar and in which she has come to understand many concepts. Children are well able to use both their first and subsequent languages in their lives and in their learning, and maintaining the first language is really important both to cognitive development and to self-esteem.

2   The second statement about bilingual children being at a disadvantage is straightforwardly incorrect. It may well be true that children who speak languages other than English will take time to acquire English, but they have already learned one or more languages and with this have explored language itself as an abstract system. They have begun to think about language per se. You will see as you read on, that bilingual and multilingual children have been shown to have greater cognitive flexibility and a sensitivity to others.

3   The teaching of English to speakers of other languages is something that is debated widely and passionately. Some educationalists still believe that withdrawal groups (where children are taken out of their classes or groups) to be taught with other non-English speakers is the best way for them to learn. What actually happens is that children in such groups have no models of other children speaking fluent English. They are singled out and made to feel different and often made

3

to feel 'stupid' or inferior. The content of these small group lessons is very narrow and based on learning vocabulary. Usually the learning makes little or no sense to the children when it is not situated in anything meaningful to them.

4 The example of Thomas not being able to choose Turkish as a language to study at his secondary school illustrates that there is a hierarchy of languages offered in schools and this relates clearly to the prejudices still held in society where some languages (mainly European languages but increasingly Chinese languages) are seen as desirable and others not. Thomas wants to learn Turkish because he has many friends who are Turkish and because he often visits Turkey with his family. The school regards it as a language of little use.

5 The fifth example, looking at the attitude of one teacher at how best to teach children English as an additional language, highlights an approach that focuses on word and rote learning rather than on learning in context. Perhaps you are familiar with the work of Margaret Donaldson who talked about how important it is for young children to be able to see the point of what they are learning in order to be able to build on their previous experience. Children in the early years who learn things through meaningful activities like cooking or washing the dolls or playing in the home corner or exploring the properties of sand and water are able to see the point of what they are doing and are able to build on what they already know and can do. Children learning to point to a picture of an apple and say the word 'apple' are involved in the equivalent of completing a worksheet.

ATTITUDES TO BILINGUALISM: A PROBLEM, A RIGHT OR A RESOURCE?

Some of the statements we have just looked at describe *language as a problem*. A child in the nursery who speaks French is seen as being advantaged, whereas one who speaks Urdu is seen as having a 'problem'. This is tied to attitudes to languages and cultures which are themselves tied to racism and prejudice. Currently, in the UK, there is a growing return to a belief that assimilation is the way ahead with the majority language (English) being encouraged to the exclusion of other languages. You may have read some articles in the press recently where high school teachers are favouring a return to this. This notion arises out of the idea that bilingual pupils often experience interference between their languages and this may, indeed, be the case. But what matters is the underlying principle that home languages don't matter which implies that culture and previous experience don't matter either. All of us involved in the care and education of young children know that this cannot be so. We know how important it is for us to know as much as we can about our children's prior experience so that we can help them build on this.

At the opposite end of the spectrum are those who believe in *language as a right*. They are illustrated by the many who argue that all people should be entitled to the right to speak or read or write in their home languages. In the USA there was a famous case, cited by Baker (2006) (*Lau v. Nichols* [1994]). This concerned the rights of a Chinese-speaking boy who appealed for the right to maintain his home language. It was argued that teaching this child through the medium of English, a language he did not fully understand, infringed his right to equal educational opportunities with other American children. In 1974 the Supreme Court accepted the child's case and this led, for a time, to an increase in the number of schools offering bilingual education. After the election of the new government in South Africa in 1994 the new constitution enshrined the rights of different groups to be educated in their home languages. This arose out of an awareness that the previous apartheid regime had forced speakers of majority languages in the country to be educated in the medium of one or other of the two languages of both power and the minority – English and Afrikaans. Some people feel so passionately about language and about the rights of people to speak and maintain their languages that they talk about language genocide – which is an extremely emotive way of describing what happens when some languages either die out or are forced to die out. Supreme amongst those who feel this is the famous Finnish linguist Tove Skutnabb-Kangas.

The last area for consideration views *language(s) as a resource*. This can be explained simply as the view held by those who believe that learners knowing more than one language know more about language itself and this is an enriching thing. You may have come across examples of settings and schools which hold this view and it is exemplified by the explicit celebration of the languages and cultures of the children in the form of displays of the scripts and alphabets of the different languages; the

5

provision of books and tapes in the different languages; the practice of translating notices for parents and carers and the employment of those who speak the community languages to work with the children and their parents.

POLICIES AND PRACTICE

The United Kingdom is home to hundreds and thousands of those who come from other countries and cultures, speaking several hundred different languages. Attitudes to these people have changed over time and continue to change, often in response to the economic stability of the country at different times, to images portrayed by the media, to changing conditions throughout the world. If we go back to the 1960s – the so-called 'swinging sixties' – we find that, despite the reported progressive views of that decade, the attitudes expressed in the Plowden Report of 1967 implied that immigrant children were deprived because of their so-called 'poor home backgrounds' and because of their unfamiliarity with British culture and the English language. This, you will appreciate, is a negative and deficit view of these children and clearly sees their presence in 'our' educational system as problematic. It contains within it the idea of 'them and us' creating a feeling that not speaking English relates to 'otherness'. This, in itself, is divisive and adds to the tensions between groups in our society.

It was suggested that the way to deal with this was to make sure that these immigrants were assimilated into the host culture, that their numbers were limited by tighter immigration controls and that some children were bussed to other schools when the proportion of immigrants in any one school reached the figure of 35%! Add to this the notion that the best way of teaching these children was to segregate them into special groups or classes or even schools until they had acquired a certain level of English when they were – reluctantly – readmitted to the mainstream.

Within only eight years attitudes had changed dramatically and when the Bullock Report was published in 1975 it insisted that the cultures and the languages of all children should be regarded as significant to their development. The report emphasised the importance of educators knowing more about languages and cultures and talked about the benefits of children not only knowing but maintaining their first language or languages. With its explicit celebration of linguistic and cultural diversity it was hugely significant in building the notion of Britain as a multi-cultural society.

This more enlightened attitude to multilingualism received another boost when there was a directive from the European Commission, urging member states to ensure that children were given mother-tongue teaching in schools. This was aimed at improving the educational performance of the children of migrant workers. It was in this more positive climate that the then Department for Education set up something called the Linguistic Minorities Project in 1985 which was tasked with providing a report on the changing patterns of bilingualism in some representative areas of England. There were other encouraging initiatives, but times were about to change. Once again, economic constraints affected policy and practice. The Swann Report, published in 1985, stated that community languages should not be offered by the state through the state school system, but by communities themselves through private Saturday and Sunday schools. This, you will know, is how things stand today – with the notable exception of Wales.

In 1988 the Education Reform Act introduced the National Curriculum and paid lip service to considering ethnic and cultural diversity and developed this more fully three years later when it stated that schools needed to consider how bilingual pupils could have full access to this curriculum and to the associated assessment arrangements. It advised educators to 'consider' the value placed on languages other than English in their curricula. Since then attitudes to languages continue to fluctuate with the consequence that those funding education and care sometimes are able and willing to fund the maintenance of community languages and sometimes not. In 2000 the Nuffield Report 'Languages: the Next Generation' was published and in 2001 the Languages National Steering Group was set up to develop a policy to change perceptions and raise awareness amongst young people and the wider public of the importance of young people acquiring language skills. The outcome of this was the document 'Languages for All: Languages for Life' – a promising title, but one which encouraged the learning of languages by children at Key Stage 2 but paid scant attention to the languages which many young children already bring to school or nursery.

LOCAL POLICIES

In many urban areas, where there are large numbers of children speaking languages other than English coming to schools and nurseries and settings, the staff have come together in order to find ways of best supporting both these children in their learning and their parents in their understanding of how the educational system works. In some places this process has taken the form of developing and writing a formal policy; in others less formal structures have, nonetheless, impacted on the school's position within the community.

Here are some case studies to consider:

Ubuntu Nursery

This is a state nursery school in a large urban conurbation. The number of languages additional to English varies from time to time but is constantly at around 50. The languages themselves also vary from time to time. Ten years ago the largest language group was Somali; today it is Polish. This reflects the changing community as some people gain easier access to the UK than others.

Five years ago, when a new headteacher was appointed, she decided that the school needed to be more proactive in several things. The first was to set up a partnership with parents and this partnership was to involve a genuine dialogue between parties in order to benefit the children. The second was to be more knowledgeable about the prior learning and experience of all the children and this meant knowing more about the languages spoken by the children and their families. The third was to be more willing to discuss difficult issues with parents in order to ensure that parents could come to know more about an educational system which might be very different from that of their home countries. You will be interested to note that the headteacher had been trained as an early years specialist.

The programme started with the parents being invited to a party at the nursery and being invited to the party personally by staff members, with the support of some of the local education authority Ethnic Minority Achievement Grant (EMAG) team who were on hand to explain and interpret.

At the party a video was shown of children at play and afterwards the headteacher explained to the parents what the children were learning as they played. This was a conscious decision on the part of the staff because they had recognised that some parents felt that playing was a waste of time and wanted to be told that their children were actually learning. There was a question-and-answer session, but this was not very effective because parents were reluctant to question. On reflection about this the staff decided that language itself might be the thing making a question-and-answer session effective and so they decided to use more visual means of communication.

They got together to make a booklet about the activities on offer and what children might learn from them. The booklet was illustrated by children's drawings and examples of their early attempts at writing and by photographs. It was translated into the three main language groups at the time. Copies of the booklets were available throughout the nursery for parents to look at and any parent who wanted to could buy a copy for a small sum.

At the next staff meeting the headteacher told each member of staff that they had to compile a list of the languages spoken by the children in each class or group and also ensure that they knew which child spoke which language. They were asked to find an example of the written form of any of the languages to bring to a staff development day. Staff found this quite difficult to do but on the staff development day examples of seven different languages were brought. These were Polish (Strona główna), Greek (Κύρια Σελίδα), Turkish (Ana Sayfa), Arabic (الصفحة الرئيسية), Cantonese, Bengali and Gujarati (ਪੁਖਪੁਖ਼).*

The reasons for this activity were twofold. In the first place the head-teacher wanted to ensure that staff knew just which languages were spoken by the children in the school to avoid hearing comments like 'She speaks Indian'. The second was that she wanted staff to be able to recognise the visible features of the written languages. So one of the sessions was devoted to looking at the written forms of these languages and finding things about them that would be recognisable in the early writing attempts of the children. Here are some of the things said during the day:

In my last school many children spoke Urdu, and now when I look at Arabic, with lots of dots and curls, it reminds me of Urdu.

* The names of some of the languages have a phrase in brackets included to show what some of the scripts and alphabets look like.

9

That line across the top of the Bengali is very distinctive and I have often seen children putting lines like that in their early writing.

Polish and Turkish use the same alphabet that we do. In Turkish there are some extra things like dots over some of the letters.

Cantonese is easy to recognise. I think those things that we call letters are called ideograms and they represent a whole word or idea.

When I see Greek writing – I've been to Greece on holiday – it always makes me think of triangles and things like that.

You can see that this nursery school is working hard to come to know more about languages and also to work more closely with parents.

Mahatma Gandhi Primary School

This primary school adopted a different, although ideologically similar, approach. They decided to have a written policy which addressed all issues of discrimination, prejudice and injustice. They considered the needs of boys and girls, and of children with special educational needs, and the very particular needs of those having English as an additional language. The policy contained this statement, which was also translated into the main languages of the school and sent home to all parents, and displayed prominently in all classrooms and around the school.

Mahatma Gandhi Primary School's Position on Bilingualism

We see bilingualism as a positive attribute which brings richness to the learning of all children.

We will encourage children to maintain and use their home and community languages throughout all areas of the curriculum.

We will encourage children to talk, to read and to write in any or all of their languages.

We will invite children to share their own experiences – social, cultural and language – with their peers and the adults in school.

We will never underestimate a child's abilities because the child has little or no English vocabulary yet.

We will ensure that children who are acquiring English are able to do this alongside their English peers, in situations which make human sense to them.

We will ensure that we are able to show the languages of the children in the displays on the walls and in the books and resources we use.

We will ensure that notices to go home are translated into the main languages of our communities.

We will ensure that translators and interpreters are available on parents' days and other events.

Because we value the children we also value the cultures and languages they bring with them.

Leafy Lane Primary School

Our last example comes from another primary school, one which is set in a leafy suburb and where there are few children who are speakers of English as an additional language, but one which is committed to helping children become members of a multicultural and multilingual world. This is the statement they have in their school booklet, which goes to all prospective and new parents.

Leafy Lane Primary School: Our children; our world

Our children are fortunate to be growing up in a world which is enriched by speakers of many languages, from many different parts of the world, having had many different experiences. In order for our children to benefit from this richness we are determined that they shall understand more about difference and diversity in order that they grow up without racism or prejudice, open to all that our cultures have to offer. In order to do this we will ensure that we have many resources to show the range of cultures, experiences, artefacts and languages that children in this country have. This means having books in English and in other languages; tapes of stories in English and other languages; tapes of music from different cultures; examples of different scripts to display on the walls; and so on. In addition we will ensure that our curriculum reflects diversity so that when we bake we might sometimes bake Turkish bread or chapattis and the dressing-up clothes will allow children to try and be not only characters from stories and from their imaginations but characters from different times and places. To ensure that this is more than tokenism we will respond promptly and urgently to any comments made by children or adults which imply that some groups are better or worse than others.

SUMMARY

In this opening chapter we have looked at multiculturalism and seen how views about its advantages or disadvantages change over time as conditions within the country change. We have looked, briefly, at some of the myths and misconceptions that have grown up around this complex issue and at the perceived hierarchy of languages. We have taken a quick tour of policies to examine how they have developed, and ended the chapter with some examples of policies developed by schools and settings to reflect their own concerns and interests.

GLOSSARY

Abstract system	Language is called an abstract system because it is made up of symbols rather than of objects.
Assimilation	This is where people who have come from another culture are expected to become like the people of the country they have come to in order to fit in.
Bilingualism	When people speak two languages.
Cognitive flexibility	The ability to make links between the things being learned. Those who have already learned more than one language are thought to be able to do this.
Community languages	The languages used by many of our children within their homes and communities.

Deficit view	A deficit view is a negative view. When people think that children who do not yet speak English are stupid they are adopting such a view. They are making unfair assumptions about ability on the basis of one aspect of learning.
Host culture	The host culture is the main culture of the country – so the host culture of England is that of England.
Ideogram	This is a character in some scripts where marks are made to represent a whole idea. Ideograms are sometimes called pictograms.
Ideological	Refers to what people value and believe.
Language genocide	A few people use this term to describe the dying-out of some languages. The implication is that languages which represent minority groups are sometimes forced out by those in power.
Learning in context	This is the learning that takes place through activities or situations where children can see the purpose of what they are doing and where they can build on what they already know. It is really the precursor of abstract learning – i.e. it should come before abstract learning.
Linguistic diversity	Where there are many different languages. Similarly cultural diversity would refer to a range of cultures.
Mother-tongue teaching	This is the term used for teaching children in the languages of their homes and communities.
Multilingualism	Refers to those who speak and may read and write three or more languages.
Rote learning	Rote learning is when learners learn things off by heart through repetition. It is learning without meaning.

Chapter 2

Language at home and beyond

In this chapter we look at the importance of language for learning, including looking closely at the importance of children's monologues and inner speech.

We look, too, at children learning and using a second language.

We explore how children both mix and switch languages and the importance of this.

The chapter ends with looking at the learning of English as a second or subsequent language.

LANGUAGE FOR LEARNING: INNER SPEECH AND SOCIAL SPEECH

It seems obvious to us that language is vital for learning and for thinking. Ours is such a language-dependent culture that we find it difficult to conceive of ways of learning and thinking that do not depend on language. Vygotsky was someone who regarded language itself as crucial to learning. In his famous book *Thought and Language*, published in English in 1986, he went beyond the views of Jean Piaget (whose work you may well have encountered) and said that language actually structures and controls the process of thinking. What he meant was that young children use language itself to help them make concepts. Piaget had thought that children used language to describe concepts already formed at a nonverbal level. Figure 1 shows the child, out in the rain, experiencing

Figure 1

'wet'. In Piaget's view the child is exploring the concept of 'wetness' through actually getting wet and not through language.

For Vygotsky language was the social means of thinking. If you think about that – and it is quite difficult to think about – you will realise that he was saying that young children learn language from others in their culture and society (that is, the social aspect of it) and that this language is what enables the child to actually develop concepts.

For Vygotsky, the child in Figure 2 is also getting wet in the rain, but is able to explore the concept of 'wet' more effectively through the language used by the mother to explain what is happening. We see how language, in this example, is the social means of thinking.

Vygotsky conceded that speech and thought were present from birth and appear to have different roots. Yet by the age of about 2 children bring the two processes together. It is then that language becomes the tool of thought – the thing that makes children able to change or

Figure 2

15

transform their understanding. This is important for anyone working with young children. The very fact of speech being the tool of transforming thinking makes us pay much more attention to the things that children say either to themselves or to others. The child in our figure understands that putting on a hat will stop her hair from getting wet, for example. So 'wet' carries with it many other concepts, some of which require action.

You may have encountered young children who speak out aloud as they do things. We call this speech 'monologues' or 'egocentric speech'. These monologues are not merely examples of children talking to themselves: rather they mark a significant moment in the development of thought. What happens is that the child, through using speech to explain or describe or question actions, begins to internalise this speech and the monologue then becomes what we sometimes call 'inner speech' or verbal thinking. There are some lovely examples in the literature of young children's monologues – being used to regulate or control their actions and to develop intellectually – becoming almost incomprehensible to adults. Here is an example taken from Gardner (1993):

A three year old is trying to count eight items and counts 'One, two, three, four, eight, ten, eleben. No, try dat again. One! Two! Three-e-four-five, ten, eleben . . . One! Two, three, four, five, six, seven, eleben, whew!'

In her work Manjula Datta (2000) looked at the significance of inner speech for bilingual learners. She noted that young children's use of language does not depend wholly on the immediate situation since the child is able to talk about what happened yesterday or what might happen tomorrow. To do this the child must be able to recall and to predict. This is the beginning of verbal thinking – talk to validate thought – and is a significant development for all young learners. For bilingual learners, using words and structures of a second language requires considerable cognitive skills. It is important that these learners are given time and opportunity to *listen* in order to tune into the sounds and the grammatical structures and patterns of their new language in different situations and contexts. Having developed inner speech in their mother tongue they also need to develop it in their second or subsequent language or languages.

Bilingual children may encounter some difficulties in recall and prediction in that the absence of objects or cues requires them to be more abstract or representational in their use of language. This may be because they have not had the same experiences as monolingual learners. Those with English as a first language may have had many experiences with other English speakers allowing them to play with language. We are thinking here of the sorts of language experiences young English-speaking children have at home or with carers involving things like nursery rhymes, finger-plays, prediction games, songs – all in English. Bilingual learners, although probably having had such experiences in their first language, may not have had them in their second or subsequent languages. Datta suggests that this may cause a gap in their ability to use inner speech in this second language.

The implications of this for those working with multilingual children are clear.

 All children should be immersed in activities which allow them to wallow in language – in playing with the sounds, with rhyme, with pattern, with intonation and so on.

The ways in which we develop auditory memory for the sounds we hear in our language come about through our experiences. Wherever you are born, into whatever language or culture, you hear around you a medley of sounds. Infants tune in to these sounds and begin to be able to identify the patterns and particular sounds that make up the language they hear most – their first language or languages. Adults support this in many ways, through the games they play involving turn-taking and prediction, through using intonation, facial expression, gesture and so on. The infant comes to know that language – or communication – is a *shared activity* and there is a strong element of *mutuality* in it. The interpersonal nature of language exchanges is predominant and it is this which allows us to talk of the first learning as social speech – which may involve no speaking in the normal sense but involves a huge amount of communicational exchanges.

It is out of this that inner speech – which could be called speech for oneself – develops. Datta tells us that some bilingual children can take part in making monologues using both their languages. She gives the example of 4-year-old Hakan who was practising counting in twos first in English and then in Turkish and then in English again. And he did this whilst running up and down the stairs (2000: 234). In the same section Datta offers the example of 3-year-old Nitya newly arrived in England and whilst travelling in the car going through a litany of the names of animals, using Hindi and the few words of English she had just acquired.

Children's monologues, then, tell us much about language acquisition and the importance of experience for fluency in a language.

Datta suggests that it tells us these things:

- language is recalled best when it is meaningful, is pleasurable and flows naturally in a meaningful context;
- young children can store speech as sequences of sounds in grammatical and often rhythmical structures and these help the development of verbal memory.

LEARNING AND USING SECOND AND SUBSEQUENT LANGUAGES: AN INTRODUCTION

Much has been written about how children acquire and use second and subsequent languages and it will not surprise you that views on this – as on many other things – change over time. We will look very briefly at the ideas of some of the most highly regarded theorists in the field, starting with Jim Cummins (1980). He used the analogy of an iceberg to help describe his thoughts.

Figure 3 An iceberg: drawing by Hannah Gardiner

An iceberg has peaks above the waterline and a body submerged below this line. When we speak of bilingualism, each peak reflects the surface features of the two languages – namely the vocabulary and the grammar. Below the waterline is where the central operating system is located. We cannot see or hear it but it controls both languages. So above the water are things like speaking and reading and writing and so on. Below the waterline is thinking.

This analogy shows the language in use above the waterline with the underlying central operating system below the waterline. What we can see and hear is the child speaking or reading or writing or listening in one or more languages. What we can't see is the thinking involved in this. So, for bilingual learners, where there are two or more languages, there is only one central operating system. This, according to Cummins, means that there is only *one integrated source of thinking*. So a common source for the thinking involved in speaking and listening, reading and writing exists.

Cummins believed that whatever language is in use at any time there is an underlying central operating system which is where the thinking that accompanies speaking, listening, reading and writing is situated. This means that when a person has access to two languages there is only one integrated source of thinking. The same applies to someone with three or more languages. This is the largest part of the iceberg and lies below the surface. Above the surface are the features of the two or more languages which are visible and evident – the vocabulary, the use of the grammatical structures of the language and so on. Cummins called his theory the model of common underlying proficiency (CUP) and said that it explained how the ability to process information and to succeed academically could be developed in two or more languages as well as in one. Cognitive functioning and school achievement might be fed through one language or through both since they both use the same underlying processor.

 The importance of this for educators is to remember that the language a child is using in the classroom needs to be sufficiently

19

well developed for the child to be able to process any cognitive challenges. If the child is forced to use an insufficiently developed language he or she will perform less well.

The second body of work we will look at is that of two extremely well-known and contentious researchers who looked at what was happening to the Finnish-speaking children of migrant workers in Sweden. These children were failing in school and Skutnabb-Kangas and Toukomaa (1988) examined the reasons for this failure. They concluded that these children when being educated in their mother tongue were as successful as Swedish children but when forced to learn through Swedish they began to fail. They proposed that without the maintenance of their mother tongue the children became what they called 'semilingual', speaking neither language fully and consequently having poor cognitive development and school performance. This notion of semilingualism has fallen out of favour and critics have pointed out that other factors such as poverty, status, low expectations of teachers and racism were operating in the case of the Finnish children.

Currently there are researchers working in many countries who adopt what is known as a *syncretic approach*. This means that they look at how children coming from different linguistic or cultural groups are active members of different groups and operate in many worlds. Kenner and Kress (2003) talk of the fact that all children live in simultaneous worlds and you can easily appreciate this when you think of the young child as a school pupil, the baby of the family, the favourite of Grandma, the friend of Julio, the nervous traveller and so on. In each context or situation the child brings together different aspects of experience in order to use languages and language styles that are appropriate to the situation. Monolingual children do this when they use different styles of talk with different people and in different contexts. Bilingual children have even more choices they can make. So our mythical child – let's call her Selina – speaks in a different way in class from the way she speaks to Julio in the garden or the way she speaks to her grandma or the way she speaks on the bus. And Selina, being bilingual, can also make choices in terms of which language she uses for each world. She speaks in Spanish to Julio and her grandma, but English to her dad on the bus. So Selina, like all children, not only *uses* different forms but *creates* new ones. Children using more than one language call upon a greater wealth of metalinguistic and metacognitive skills and strategies. When children can play out different roles their opportunities to refine these skills are increased. Children's understanding of which language and which style to use is *mediated* by others. These others may be parents or other adults or role models or other children. Often these models are themselves bi-cultural and/or bilingual and as mediators are able to guide children's participation, scaffold their learning or organise situations with coopera-tion and negotiation built in – as when monolingual children play with bilingual children or young children play with older children. The term often used for this is *synergy*.

 There is much to think about here in terms of offering bilingual learners many opportunities to be part of different worlds – sometimes with other speakers of their first language, sometimes as experts teaching others about their languages and sometimes learning from speakers of other languages.

LANGUAGE-MIXING AND LANGUAGE-SWITCHING

Listening to young multilingual children is fascinating because they so often mix their language using words or phrases from both or all of their languages in a single utterance. Perplexing as this may be for the listener, this is not evidence of confused thinking or inadequacy. Theorists think that what is happening is that very young children associate one lan-guage with particular people or activities or situations. In older children language-switching is a common phenomenon as more fluent multi-lingual learners change languages mid-sentence or mid-phrase. Some linguists explain this in terms of tiredness or distraction, the inability to find a particular word in one language, a sign of group solidarity or belong-ing, a device to exclude others, a way of clarifying something or an asso-ciation of some activities or concepts with one language and one culture. Gumperz (1982) tells us that code or language-switching is when speak-ers use more than one language in the course of a single speech act. You will realise that bilinguals have two sets of language sounds in their heads and their use depends on the particular contexts or purposes for talk. It seems that for bilingual children their two languages are not seen as two separate things, but they understand them as 'language' and use them interchangeably in appropriate contexts. Here are what some

21

children have said about their language use. Read the remarks to see how much they reveal about the metalinguistic skills of these children.

Celina   I speak Spanish to my grandparents when I go to their house, but I speak English to my friends at school.

Brother   I can speak isiZulu, isiXhosa and English – oh, and Afrikaans. I speak English in school but isiZulu at home and Afrikaans when we go to church. I only speak isiXhosa when I play with another child who speaks that language.

Ming Lei At home we speak English and Cantonese. I learn English at school. I am trying to learn Hindi so I can talk to my friend Farhana and she says I can learn it from Indian films.

This acute awareness of languages and their appropriateness to contexts and people is known as *communicative sensitivity*.

THE LEARNING OF ENGLISH AS A SECOND OR ADDITIONAL LANGUAGE: AN INTRODUCTION

The children we are considering are primarily those who have already acquired their first language or languages. Some children acquire two or more languages at the same time – particularly those living in families where there are adult speakers of more than one language. For these children, who acquire two or more languages simultaneously, both languages have equal cognitive and emotional weight for the child. So Amelie, learning English from her mother and French from her father, used both languages from very early on and, although each might have been more associated with certain people, in general, she used the languages interchangeably.

Many of the children we encounter in our schools and settings are those who are learning English as a subsequent language. They have already learned at least one language and are now having to learn another. Datta argues that those who are learning English as a second or subsequent language should be learning it as an additional tool and *never to replace the first or home languages*. Where attempts are made to force the pace of learning English and to deny the use of first languages by the children the first language is displaced and this can lead to what is known as *subtractive bilingualism*. This term implies a huge gap in the meanings and the schemata (repeated patterns of behaviour) and the self-image and the confidence of the learner. For any child this would be a huge load to carry and it is important that educators and practitioners remain attentive to matching the pace of English teaching to the needs of each individual child.

Those of us working with the thousands of multilingual children in our settings and schools have no doubt that these children, if they are to succeed in our educational system and our country, do need to learn English. The vexed question is how this should happen. There are many different models of children learning English (or another language) as a second or subsequent language. In some cases children are plunged into the new language, like being thrown into a swimming pool without any support and left to sink or swim (see Figure 4).

This is referred to as the submersion approach. In other models children are more gently inducted into the new language. The swimming pool analogy can be adapted to describe the children jumping into the water, but with armbands or floats provided to ensure that they don't sink (see Figure 5).

Figure 4 The child, thrown into an all-English classroom, is offered nothing to hang onto in terms of her own language or her own experience. The story of Antti (which you will encounter in the next chapter) shows his responses to this situation.

Figure 5 A child immersed in an all-English classroom but with support will not sink. The support can be use of the mother tongue, mother-tongue speakers to help, evidence of the child's language and culture being respected and so on.

This is the immersion approach. It does not require a lot of thought to recognise that a submersion approach would offer the children nothing to help them build on what they already know and would take no account of their cultural or linguistic differences and experiences. Immersion would gently bathe the children in English whilst allowing them to use their first languages.

You may have read of some of the immersion programmes such as those in Canada. Closer to home we have the example of Wales which is a bilingual country offering bilingual education where the teaching is through the medium of both Welsh and English. Here – and in other successful immersion programmes – bilingual teachers are employed and children are not made to feel different and outside of the main-stream. Of course in a country like Wales where there is one main language group other than English the situation is relatively simple. What can we, with our tens of languages in any one school, do to mimic this more sympathetic and humane approach?

There are many books you can read about this if it is of particular interest to you. We will confine ourselves to looking at some of the principles that emerge from the writing of people like Baker (2006), Kenner (2004b) and others.

These principles are summarised here:

- The *context* in which children acquire a new language matters. Language is acquired when the learner understands messages. It is not grammar or vocabulary that is learned, but meanings and messages that are exchanged. *So learning languages is social.*

- Children learn a huge amount from their *peers* and they do this through play, in meaningful activities such as eating lunch, in different contexts like in the playground and so on. *Having peer models of fluent English is a powerful way of learning.*

- Children want to be the *same as other children.* They want to speak the language of the school and of TV and of the cinema and of their friends. *This is about belonging and is an important incentive.*

- Children know a great deal about their own language and, when in situations where adults recognise and value this, can act as *peer tutors* to other children. Kenner's work on young bilingual children learning and teaching about their own and other languages offers an exciting model as do the writers in Gregory *et al.*'s book (2004) who talk about children learning with siblings, grandparents, peers and communities. You will be able to read more about this in the next chapter.

SUMMARY

In this chapter we have started thinking about language and thought and the links between them and in doing this we touched on children using monologues to say out loud or to confirm their ideas and thoughts as well as children using speech with others for social purposes. We have looked, too, at children learning first and second or subsequent languages and seen how bilingual learners learn about language itself when they learn another language. And we have seen how bilingual learners mix languages and switch languages.

CORNWALL COLLEGE
LEARNING CENTRE

GLOSSARY

Analogy	When something is compared to something else.
Auditory memory	This refers to what happens as young infants begin to be able to store and remember sounds they have heard.
Communicative sensitivity	The ability to know what style or register of language to use with different people in different contexts.
Egocentric speech	Synonymous with monologues: children using spoken language to describe and explain what they are doing or experiencing.
Immersion	This is when children are allowed to learn or acquire another language by being in situations where that language is spoken for real purposes. The child is allowed to wallow in the language.
Inner speech	This is when the monologues become internalised so that they are no longer spoken aloud but serve as thinking.
Integrated source of thinking	This term is used to describe what has been observed about how bilingual or multilingual people can use more than one language because, it is assumed, there is only one language used for thought and this is possibly made up of the strands of both or all the languages.
Interpersonal	Something that happens between two or more people.
Intonation	The ups and downs of voices in speech.
Language mixing	When bilingual children use words from more than one language in a sentence or statement.
Language shifting	When bilingual children select between their languages according to context, audience and emotional content.

Meaningful/ meaningful context	This term is used here to talk about situations which make human sense to the child and where there are opportunities to draw on what has already been learned and experienced.
Mediate	Where someone or something assists someone in achieving something.
Metacognition	This term is used to talk about knowing about knowing itself.
Metalinguistic	It follows that this term refers to knowing about language itself.
Monologue	When children say things aloud in order to help them sort out their understanding of what they are seeing, hearing or doing.
Mutuality	Where there is a strong sense of one thing affecting another to arrive at shared meaning or understanding.
Predict	To be able to say or think what will happen next; this is a higher-order cognitive skill.
Processor	In this sense, a processor is some sort of mechanism which allows the child to do something. We are talking about something that allows the child to work out, use, apply and invent the rules of language.
Recall	This means to remember or bring back to mind.
Scaffold	In this context scaffolding refers to ways in which the learner is helped to move from dependence to independence by the careful support of adults (or peers) in a gradual and positive manner.
Second language	The child's first language is the one the child hears and learns first. Second languages come afterwards.
Semilingual	A term used to describe children in the early stages of second-language acquisition which has fallen out of favour since it implies that these children are neither bilingual nor monolingual.

Shared activity	When two people focus on the same activity – a child and an adult, or two children, for example.
Social speech	This is when children use spoken language with others.
Submersion	As an approach to children learning another language this is a system which literally drops the children into situations and hopes for the best. Sink or swim!
Subsequent language	When a child learns a second language after having acquired a first language
Subtractive bilingualism	Where a learner who is forced to learn a new language too quickly experiences negative consequences.
Syncretic approach	Many theorists now consider that children are able to operate in different language systems, cultural worlds and social settings at the same time. Syncretism ascribes their abilities to speak differently to different people or in different contexts.
Synergy	The bringing together of separate views in cooperation.
Verbal thinking	Thinking involving words, often spoken aloud; can you conceive of thinking without words? Many people believe that it is possible to think without using words, and cite music, dance or painting as evidence of this.

Chapter 3

Language and identity

We start this chapter with a consideration of how we all construct our own identity and an analysis of how intimately language is tied to identity.

We then examine ways of discovering what languages are spoken by the children and their families and look at the visible features of some languages.

We look at practical ways of using first language in the classroom or setting through adapting books, making bilingual tapes, learning vocabulary, recognising scripts, using play and meaningful contexts.

We then look at some of the current studies on what bilingual children can teach other bilingual or monolingual children about language.

CONSTRUCTING IDENTITY

If you were asked the question 'What is your identity?' you might well struggle to answer it. In a sense there are as many answers to this question as there are people to answer it. Our identity is not something we were born with; not something fixed or unitary. Rather it is socially created through a complex and intricate web of interactions and negotiations and relationships, and mediated by language. Each new experience or context allows us to re-create and reconstruct our identity. Here are what some students, in a group discussion, said about identity:

I am an American. I was born there. But my parents both came from Ireland and I heard tales about Ireland and Irish stories, both true and made up. So part of my identity is Irish. Part is American and I guess part is becoming British. Part is also daughter – the daughter of my parents. And part is student – student at the university. And part is friend. I could go on forever.

My identity? So difficult to define. I love being a Bengali speaker. It is such an expressive language and it links me to the people I love most in all the world. But there have been times when I hated that people just saw me as that – as a bilingual, a foreigner, an immigrant. People don't see that I was born here and that I love lots that is English – the language, the literature, the films. So it is complicated.

I like that I can be a different person in different contexts. Like yours, my identity is tied up with where I am and who I am with and how they react to me. When I first started this course I was very shy and wouldn't speak up. I was a fluent English speaker, although often I thought in Urdu. Now, having established myself with all of you – my peers – I am more confident and present myself differently. Yet take me to a party and I will go back into my shell. I guess my identity changes according both to how I am treated and how I expect to be treated. As someone from a minority culture I am always wary of the responses I will get.

Language is a symbol of our identity but it does not, on its own, define us. We have seen from the statements above how our identities change according to context. Baker (2006) tells us that we do not own one identity but rather make and adopt multiple identities according to where we are and who we are with. Part of this flexibility involves what Rampton (1995) called '*language crossing*' where, in his account, young men borrow and use phrases from the languages of their peers. You can see this phenomenon not only with languages but with music (the violinist Yehudi Menuhin adapting classical music when playing with instrumentalists from other cultures) and film (Hollywood vs. Bollywood) and cooking (Italian pizzas with chilli con carne topping), for example. One of the things that affects identity is immigration. Eva Hoffman, a young bilingual, wrote an autobiographical account of what happened to her when she became an immigrant. The book is called *Lost in Translation: A Life in a New Language* (1989) and is published by Dutton. Eva Hoffman was born in Cracow, Poland, and emigrated to Canada in the late 1950s with her family. In the book she explores what she saw and heard and felt as a newcomer into an alien culture and charts with precision and sensitivity how she quickly learned English, but in the process lost some Polish and with it some of her identity. In an interview in 2000, she said, 'I think every immigrant becomes a kind of amateur anthropologist – you do notice things about the culture or the world that you come into that people who grow up in it, who are very embedded in it, simply don't notice. I think we all know it from going to a foreign place. And at first you notice the surface things, the surface differences. And gradually you start noticing the deeper differences. And very gradually you start with understanding the inner life of the culture, the life of those both large and very intimate values. It was a surprisingly long process is what I can say.'

If we are not born with our identity fixed, it follows that we must construct it for ourselves. We do this through many means. From birth children start to construct their identities from their experiences and through their interactions. This includes seeing themselves as part of a group sharing a culture. The ways in which they and other members of their group are perceived and represented will be crucial in doing this. So children construct their identities partially from how they (the group) are represented. It will feel very different being the only black child in an all-white class, or being the only girl on the football team, for example. How children define and identify themselves is a complex process and one that essentially involves their self-esteem. The reactions of others to them or to their group impact on their self-image and hence on their self-identity. Children who encounter few images or predominantly negative images of themselves and their group will suffer damage to their self-esteem and the whole process of identity construction will be difficult.

In *Minority Education: From Shame to Struggle* (Skutnabb-Kangas and Cummins, 1988), Antti Jalava wrote a piece called 'Nobody could see that I was a Finn'. In this disturbing autobiographical piece he wrote about his experiences after his family moved from Finland to Stockholm when he was 9 years old. On the first day at school the principal did not know what to do with this little stranger: all she could do was hold the child's hand as they walked to the classroom . . .

31

Holding hands was the only language we had in common.

In class the child was called names and teased. He tried to adjust:

Adjusting was not, however, at all simple. To what did one have to adjust and how? There was nobody to explain things, there were no interpreters, no Finnish teachers and no kind of teaching of the Swedish language. And I was no chameleon, either, for I only wanted to be myself, out of habit and instinct. When the others wrote in Swedish, I wrote in Finnish. But that was something that just couldn't be. The teacher grabbed my pencil and angrily shook his finger at me. In spite of everything I continued to fall back on my mother tongue.

When you read that, you get a really strong sense of the child's struggle both to become part of the new host culture (Sweden and school) but also to retain part of his self-identity (his language). Writing in Finnish is a clear sign of his need to do this. As the children in the class wrote in Swedish Antii did the only thing that was possible for a child who clearly had the capacity to understand the task together with the implied rules and conventions, but was not equipped with the tool of knowing the language (Swedish) – which proved to be the essential tool. The child ended up in the office of the principal and that night threw a stone through the window of the principal's office and never again wrote in Finnish. He bonded with a band of what he called 'brothers' and said that violence became the only language understood by all of them. By the time he moved up to the junior grades he had learned some Stockholm slang and said that the language of the classroom, which he described as middle-class Swedish, was as impenetrable to the working-class Swedish boys as it was to him. He was fiercely homesick and went down to the docks to watch the boats from Finland come and go. He wept in private. But with time the idea grew within him that it was shameful to be a Finn. The way in which he writes about this is powerful and painful:

Everything I had held dear and self-evident had to be destroyed. An inner struggle began, a state of crisis of long duration. I had trouble sleeping. I could not look people in the eye, my voice broke down into a whisper, I could no longer trust anybody. My mother tongue was worthless – this I realized at last; on the contrary it made me the butt of abuse and ridicule . . . So down with the Finnish language! I spat on myself, gradually committed internal suicide . . . I resolved to learn Swedish letter perfect so nobody could guess who I was or where I came from.

You can see how difference and prejudice can operate against groups and also within groups. This child made the terrible decision to give up his language and become as perfect in Swedish as it was possible to be, precisely in order to disguise his true identity as an individual and his identity as part of a group. His words – *gradually committed internal suicide* – powerfully illustrate the depths of his despair.

There is much for those involved with young children to consider in this and we will turn our attention to some of this now.

 ## KNOWING THE LANGUAGES OF THE CHILDREN

It is essential for all educators to know which languages are spoken by the families of the children in their care. More than that, it is important to know what the alphabets and scripts of the languages look like and extremely helpful to learn some basic phrases in as many of the languages as possible. Finding out about the languages spoken at home can be done through talking to the children themselves, to their older siblings, to their parents or through finding other parents or older children who may speak the same language. In many schools and settings this vital information is gathered on admission alongside information about the child's previous experiences, likes and dislikes and position in family, for example.

Displaying some recognition of the languages in the class or the group is a small token of respect and goes some way to indicate to all children and all families a respect for linguistic diversity. There are many welcome posters available which use some of the main languages in this country and it is also possible – and often better – to make your own, asking local translators, or parents or older children, to write something simple for you to display. Here are some examples drawn from schools and settings shown here in English only, but made available in many other languages.

Welcome to our class

This is the reception class.

The teacher's name is . . . .

The classroom assistant speaks . . . .

We would like you to visit us on Monday mornings.

Learning some phrases in other languages is something worth doing, particularly where you are working with very young children. What phrases you feel you need to learn will vary and may range from the very simple, like a greeting, to the more complicated, like 'Don't cry' or 'Toilet?' It is also worthwhile asking speakers of the languages in your group if they can teach you some songs and rhymes and you can teach these to all the children. This overt sharing of languages is something that shows the children that songs can be sung and rhymes chanted in all languages and this is an important part of helping them come to understand that all languages can be used equally effectively for communication and understanding. Another thing that is relatively simple to do is to learn to write and say numbers from 1 to 10 in the main languages of your group.

Here are some examples of good practice relating to the use of languages in addition to English.

At *Leafy Lane Primary School* there is:

1   a welcome poster in the nursery and it displays many languages even though the school is monolingual.
2   a very keen and thoughtful nursery teacher who has taken the trouble to learn to count to five in Urdu. She plans to do this for the coming term and then perhaps choose another language in the following term. She is very concerned that what she is doing makes some sense to the children and doesn't want it to be tokenist. So she is also planning to display the Urdu script in the graphics area and to read stories to the children about Pakistan.
3   some attention paid to offering the children artefacts and books and images to help reflect the wider multicultural world. The nursery teacher has put some saris in the

dressing-up area together with cooking utensils which she bought at a local shop. She says: 'It is very difficult in a school like this to do anything that is meaningful for the children in terms of multilingualism, but I feel that it is important because we all live in a multilingual world. I do what I can but fear that it is too little and not sufficiently embedded in the lives of the children. I was really pleased to meet the new school nurse, who comes from Pakistan, and I asked her to come into my class to tell the children about her life and her work. In fact it was meeting her that made me choose Urdu for this term.'

At *Mahatma Gandhi Primary School* the approach is more integrated and this is because this is a school where the majority of children have English as an additional language. They provide many things to celebrate linguistic diversity, such as:

1   Their policy on multicultural education, which you have already encountered (in the first chapter)
2   A large book made by staff and illustrated with photographs, which show some of the things the children do throughout the day. The book shows children playing in the garden and in the playground, eating lunch, building with blocks, pretending to write, listening to stories, looking at books and playing musical instruments.
3   Signs up to help parents and visitors find their way round the school
4   Photographs up of all the people who work in the school together with labels saying what their roles are
5   In all the classrooms there are books in English and other languages and all children regularly take home books to share.
6   Home corners, available in all the Foundation Stage and Key Stage 1 classrooms, have a range of artefacts and cooking utensils and dressing-up clothes to allow children to see familiar objects from their homes.
7   Letters that go home to parents are translated by the local authority translation unit.

8 Attention is paid to the timing of open days so that lone parents and working parents can attend and translators are always available.

9 The school takes trouble to employ as many speakers of the community languages in the school as possible as teachers, nursery nurses, teaching assistants, meals supervisors and others.

10 Parents and carers are invited to come into all the classrooms on a regular basis to support the children.
The headteacher sums it up by saying: 'We want all parents and carers to know, from day one, that their language and culture is important to us. We feel this very strongly because we know how important it is for all children to be able to build on what they already know and not have to leave their language and culture at the school gate.'

You need to know about the languages of the children for another reason and that is to better enable you to understand the early attempts children make to become writers. As you may well know, young children explore what they can do when making marks and begin to try to use mark-making to communicate and share meanings. In their earliest attempts children move from making marks that appear to be no more than the result of their attempts to move their hands across a piece of paper with a pencil or crayon or paintbrush used as an extension of their hands. But after a while an examination of the marks children make leads us to be able to interpret what it is they are trying to do. Often what they do is to draw on their own experience – in this case on the experience they have had of seeing words around them, seeing people in their communities read, looking at books and so on. There has been a considerable body of research into early writing and one of the things that emerges is that there is a focus on signs. In other words children pay attention to writing as a system of signs and to how the features of these signs are arranged. So they examine how the marks are aligned on the page, the direction in which they are written and read, and the specific aspects of the written language they see in their homes and cultures. If you give a very young child a blank form it is highly probable that the child will make marks in the boxes. If you give the child a thin strip of paper it is likely the child will 'write' a list. The children use mark-making as an opportunity to experiment with what they have noticed in their lives.

Young children who have had experiences of seeing the scripts of the languages of their homes and communities will try to include these in their early attempts at writing. Hebrew and Arabic children might write from right to left. Bengali children sometimes include horizontal lines in their early writing and Urdu early writers use many curls and dots. When children begin to write words they often replicate the grammatical forms of their first language in their early writing. If you are not familiar with the shapes and orientation of the scripts of the children in your group you will not be able to recognise what it is that they are doing. And if you encounter something that seems strange to you in a child's writing it is worthwhile talking to someone who knows something about the home language of the child. In the section that follows you will find some fascinating examples illustrating what children themselves know about their home literacies.

There are a number of websites that you can access which will offer you information and ideas which you may find helpful as you become more and more confident about meeting the learning needs of all the children in your group, your class or your community. They are listed here:

- *www.standards.dfes.gov.uk/ethnicminorities*: this site contains a wide range of policy and practice documents relating to the education of pupils from minority ethnic communities. The site links to the NLS revised edition of *Supporting Pupils Learning English as an Additional Language*, which has highly recommended advice on practice as well as video clips.
- *www.cre.gov.uk*: the website of the Commission for Racial Equality, and useful for legislation and publications
- *www.qca.org.uk*: the site of the Qualifications and Curriculum Authority and where you can find documents like 'A Language in Common'
- *www.naldic.org.uk/ITTSEAL*: this is the website of the National Association for Language Development in the Curriculum, the professional association of teachers and others specifically working with children who have English as an additional language. The ITTSEAL section is specifically aimed at Initial Teacher Education.

▶ *www.multiverse.ac.uk*: this site contains a wide range of recommended on-line material on issues of diversity such as race and ethnicity, social class, religion, bilingual learners, travellers and refugees. It has been designed for the needs of those training to become teachers and for those new to teaching.

▶ *www.standards.dfes.gov.uk/keystage3/strands*: this site gives access to a range of documents which give guidance on supporting bilingual learners in all main subjects of the National Curriculum at Key Stage 3 (KS3).

YOUNG BILITERATE EXPERTS: CHILDREN TEACHING OTHERS ABOUT THEIR LANGUAGES

There is a growing body of evidence illustrating just how much young children know about their own languages and about language itself. The term used to describe knowledge about language itself is *meta-linguistic awareness*. Gregory *et al.* (2004) tell us that all children are members of different cultural and linguistic groups and actively seek to belong to these groups in a way which is not linear but is dynamic, fluid and changing. More than that, children do not remain in the separate worlds defined by their cultural group, but move between worlds. It is as though they live in *'simultaneous' worlds*. This is a phrase used by Kenner and Kress (2003). Think of a child you know and you will realise that the child is a member of the cultural group of her or his family but also is actively creating the cultural group of her or his setting or classroom. And, as members of different groups, children, often in their play, transform or change the languages and narrative styles, the role relationships and learning styles appropriate to each group and then change the cultures and languages they use to create new forms. These are complex ideas. Let us illustrate them with some examples to show these ideas in action.

The first example comes from the work of Charmian Kenner (2004a and 2004b). Working in a South London nursery class she observed bilingual children giving evidence of using both of their languages in their examples of mark-making. She cites the example of 4-year-old Meera who used both Gujarati and English scripts in most of her texts. When Meera chose to make a travel brochure it was about India (where her grandparents lived) and for that she said, 'I want to write my Gujarati' and proceeded to make marks with the characteristics of written Gujarati. You can see how this child verbalised her decision to select Gujarati in order to 'write' in the travel brochure about the country of her grandparents. She matched her language to her perceived audience and context.

Another researcher, Aura Mor-Sommerfield (2002), found examples of young children using features of both their languages (Hebrew and English) in the same text and coping with the differences in the directionality of the two scripts through inventive ways of making the scripts snake across the page – left to right and then right to left and back again. You will know that English is read from left to right across the page and Hebrew is read from right to left. These children were only 6 years old yet they arrived at creative solutions to a problem they encountered. Mor-Sommerfield gave this process the descriptive name of '*language mosaic*' and it is essentially the same process used by bilingual children in speaking when they switch languages. Switching and mixing of language and aspects of language is something often seen in emergent bilinguals.

Abdul-Hayee Murshad, researching the verbal language use of bilingual Bengali/English children in the playground of a London school, noticed that not only did they switch vocabulary but also seemed to be creating a new kind of grammar, drawing on the structures of both languages.

These examples illustrate how some of those children, fortunate enough to interact in cross-linguistic (where more than one language is involved) and cross-cultural (where more than one culture is involved) practices are able to call on a wider range of *metacognitive* and *metalinguistic* strategies (a reminder that metacognitive means the ability to think about thinking itself; metalinguistic means knowledge about language itself). These strategies are further enhanced when the children are able to play out different roles. In any role they play they are involved in interactions and often there is some mediation where the mediators are usually bilingual. Mediators may be peers or adults.

There is much evidence to show that children learn to decode and interpret the particular graphic sign systems (the alphabets or scripts) used by the culture(s) in which they live. Children who see others writing from left to right will tend to copy that. Those seeing others make marks with a continuous line running above each symbol will tend to copy that. We know that these signs are socially constructed and that children make meaning from these through their interactions. So children see adults writing letters or notes or lists or postcards or marks in a register and in their role-playing try to interpret the purposes of the marks as well as their style. Some of the most exciting recent research looks at how, when children are able to play the role of 'teacher', they begin to reinterpret their own understanding in order to explain it to their peers. When you read through the examples that follow, try and see what the children have found out about their language – spoken or written.

Kenner (2004a) looked at what some 6-year-old bilingual children were doing at a community Saturday school where they were learning to write in their family language whilst learning literacy in English at their primary school. Peer teaching sessions were set up so that the children could teach one another how to write in Chinese or in Arabic or in Spanish – three languages with very different graphic systems. Here is an extract from what happened when Tala tried to teach Emily to write a word in Arabic – a language with which Emily was not familiar. Tala wanted to teach Emily to write her brother's name, Khalid. This is written in two parts, one for each syllable, because, according to the rules of Arabic writing, the letters 'alif' (which represent the 'a' sound) cannot join to any following letter. Tala wrote the word herself, in front of Emily, telling her what she was doing.

'Do that – it's like a triangle, but it's got a line like here . . . go "wheee" like this' (as she finished with an upward stroke). Emily tried to follow this lead, saying as she wrote 'It looks like an "L" . . . it looks like steps.' As Amina had done with Chinese, Emily was interpreting an unfamiliar script from the basis of English and of visual images. However, Tala realized that Emily had over-interpreted her instructions, with the result being too stylized and she commented 'It's not exactly like that – she's done steps.' Indeed, Emily's version looked like steps in a staircase rather than the fluid curves typical of Arabic writing. This difficulty continued during the lesson and to help her friend produce more appropriate writing, Tala resorted to a technique used by her own Arabic teacher. She provided a 'join-the-dots' version of the words required.

(Kenner, 2004a: 113)

Tala knows a great deal about how the characters are formed. She under-stands some of the rules. More than that, she is able to explain to her friend Emily, what is going wrong with Emily's attempts to write an Arabic letter. How resourceful of Tala to recognise that what she can do to help Emily is what her Arabic teacher did to help her.

Another example showed Yazan writing an Arabic word using the work he did in his Saturday school as a model. As he wrote he com-mented on what he was doing, saying things like 'This looks like a zero' or 'This looks like a one'. All these observations using the words 'looks like' indicate his awareness of the fact that there are simi-larities between the Arabic symbols and the English numerals but also an awareness that they do not refer to the same things. The deep knowledge revealed by this shows that this 6-year-old knows that similar symbols can coexist in different writing systems.

Sadhana revealed that she could not only think in both of her languages, Spanish and English, but even use both in the same word. Kenner tells us that this happened when she was at home with her mother, using some cardboard alphabet letters to form English words in one list with Spanish words against them in another list.

> Sadhana was making the word 'girl' in English which would then be followed by its equivalent in Spanish, 'nina'. She put out the letters g-e-r (she was representing the way girl is pronounced in English which sounds more like gel or gerl).
>
> When her mother asked 'What else?' because the word was un-finished Sadhana said 'Nina. We're missing A' and added an 'a' to the letters she had already set out, making 'gera'. She then immedi-ately said 'No, girl! I'm doing a girl, girl' and started looking for the letter 'l' instead which would complete the English word.
>
> (Kenner, 2004a: 115)

It does not take much to realise just how much this child already knew about languages. She understood that one concept could be expressed by different words and she was able to explore the differences in the two systems, realising that the 'a' on the end of 'nina', which signifies a feminine article, does not ever apply in English and as soon as she had added the 'a' to her word recognised that it did not look correct. If you are interested in this, Kenner's book is fascinating and not difficult to read.

41

In *Many Pathways to Literacy* (2004) (edited by Eve Gregory, Susi Long and Dinah Volk) there are numerous examples of children teaching one another and learning from one another. Here is an example of three children playing school. It is taken from Ann Williams's piece called 'Playing School in Multiethnic London'. Wahida is 10 and Sayeda is 8 years old.

Wahida	Now we are going to do homophones. Who knows what homophone is? No one? OK. I'll tell you one and then you're going to do some by yourselves. Like watch. One watch is your time watch, like 'What's the time' watch: and another watch is 'I'm watching you. I can see you . . .' So Sayeda, you wrote some in your books haven't you? Can you please tell me some, please. Can you only give me three, please.
Sayeda	Oh. I wanted to give you five.
Wahida	No, Sayeda, we haven't got enough time. We've only got five minutes to assembly.
Sayeda	Son is the opposite of daughter . . . And sun is . . . It shines on the sky so bright . . .

(Williams, 2004: 63)

Can you see how Wahida is using the language of the classroom and the intonation patterns used by the teachers? She is clearly in control and inducts her younger sister not only into the mysteries of homophones but into the practices and the specific language of school.

In the same book Susi Long, Donna Bell and Jim Brown look at how children can support their peers through interaction. Here is a teaching assistant, Ms Alvarez, reading an English picture book to a small group of Spanish-speaking children, including Marcial, who is a beginner learner of English, and Maya, who is a Spanish/English bilingual. At one point Ms Alvarez stopped reading to ask the children to describe an illustration.

Ms Alvarez	Tell me what you see here.
Marcial	(Looks closely at the illustration)
Ms Alvarez	What do you see here?
Marcial	(Looks confused)

Maya	Que ve usted aqui? What do you see? (Maya translates Ms Alvarez's question into Spanish and then she says it again in English.)
Ms Alvarez	Tell me about the picture.
Maya	He is looking.
Ms Alvarez	Marcial, what do you see here?
Marcial	Hay un chico y un perro. (There's a boy and a dog.)
Maya	He sees a boy and a dog.

(Long, Bell and Brown, 2004: 99)

These children are 8 years old and from this brief extract you get a real sense of how much support a bilingual peer can offer. Maya is able to interpret what Marcial needs in order to respond to the questions. She can translate the teaching assistant's questions and Marcial's replies and she can act as go-between in the sense of reminding the teaching assistant that the child needs time to look before responding. More than that, she translates Marcial's response not literally but in terms of what he said.

WHAT DO WE LEARN FROM THIS?

1   Children who are *alongside other speakers of their language* can turn to them for support in making sense of new situations. Adults working with bilingual children need to be alert to this and sometimes pair up or group children to allow this to happen.

2   Children who are *asked to show their knowledge*, their expertise in terms of their own language, find themselves in the position of teacher and in that role are able to reveal their own, often complex, understanding of aspects of language per se. Adults working with children should engineer situations within the class or setting to facilitate this.

3   Children *learn from all those around them* and they continue to learn within their homes (from parents and grandparents and siblings), and at any out-of-school settings they attend (like Saturday or Sunday schools). Adults working with bilingual children need to remember this and expect bilingual children to be experts in their home language(s).

43

4   Children need many *opportunities for playing a range of roles* which they choose and in these roles can explore the different purposes and contexts and audiences using either or both of their languages. Any bilingual classroom should provide for this through role play areas, the reading of stories, drama and storytelling.

5   Where those working with children show that they know that some of the children are speakers (and sometimes readers and writers) of other languages and show respect both for the languages and for the skills of the children, a genuine multilingual culture can grow within the class or the setting.

SUMMARY

In this important chapter we have considered the ties between language and identity: we are, at least partially, defined by the languages we speak and the cultures we belong to. The implications of this are clear for those of us working with children and we moved on to looking at why (and how) we can learn as much as possible about the languages of our children and show, explicitly, our respect for them. To illustrate just what it is that young bilinguals know about language itself through becoming bilingual we have looked at some recent research. The chapter closes with some 'tips for teachers' in the sense that it links theory/research with practice.

GLOSSARY

Cross-cultural	Where more than one culture meets another – this operates in almost all classrooms and settings in this country.
Cross-linguistic	Where more than one language meets another.
Graphic sign system	An alphabet or a script.
Homophones	The technical term for words that sound the same.

Language crossing	This is where children or other bilinguals borrow or use words and phrases from their peers. Think about the prevalence of words like 'cool' in the spoken language of almost all young people – monolingual or not.
Language mosaic	A term used to describe the mixing of languages often observed in children – in their written and spoken work.
Mediate	To act as a go-between.
Metacognition	Understanding about learning itself.
Metalinguistic	Understanding about language itself.
Peer teaching	Where one child teaches another or others.
Simultaneous worlds	A phrase used to illustrate how children adopt different roles, languages, styles and so on in the many different contexts they find themselves in.

Chapter 4

Learning a language: learning another

What it means to learn a first language
Learning two languages at once
Learning a second or subsequent language

In this chapter we examine what is currently known about how all children acquire their first language and how many of them acquire a second or subsequent language. We look at the differences there are between these two types of learning and also at what children must do in order to become fully bilingual. Finally we examine what changes there have been in legislation in this country.

LEARNING A FIRST LANGUAGE

From very early on human infants show a unique communicative pattern of behaviour. They begin to indicate the need to have things labelled or named for them. They do this by looking at or pointing to or holding up objects, inviting others to share attention and provide the label.

Children begin using linguistic symbols (sounds and words, for example) in order to communicate. There is almost certainly some imitation involved as the child repeats words used by adults, internalises the sounds heard and then makes those same sounds in order to make and share meaning. Imitation may be part of the story but there are questions to be asked and answered in order to know whether it, alone, is enough. Ask yourself if you think it possible for mere imitation to account for children being able to say things they will never have heard anyone else say. Keep this question in your mind as you read on.

Some people believe that in order to understand how language is learned or acquired we must be able to regard *talk* itself to be a symbolic act. Often people think of symbols being things that can be seen or touched or held or moved. Talk consists of sounds and these are not random or haphazard but combined in particular ways in order to represent things. Names or nouns represent or stand for objects or people and these are the first linguistic symbols children use. If you have children of your own you will probably remember the first recognisable 'words' they used and will, perhaps, agree that these were names for things or people. Nouns are then combined with other words in order to create strings of words which build into phrases and sentences. Language is rule-bound so that the ways in which words can be combined in order to create meaning are apparent and are clearly understood by language users. But language is not fixed and static. New words come into languages and some words drop out of languages. You may have seen a recent showing of the programme *49Up* on television and heard a 7-year-old in the year 1963 say, 'My heart's desire is to see my father.' This is a phrase almost unknown in the spoken language of today. Not only is language fluid and changing but it is also creative. Children play with language just as they play with objects.

> Sammy, at the age of 5, looked at her sister sitting across from her at the table and commented, 'She is oppositting me.' She has made a new verb by combining words and concepts – sitting and opposite.

This shows a child making up words according to the ways in she perceives words to work.

> 'Twas brillig, and the slithy toves
> Did gyre and gimble in the wabe;
> All mimsy were the borogoves,
> And the mome raths outgrabe.

This is from that master of playful language, Lewis Carroll, from one of the poems in *Through the Looking-Glass*.

The notion that children acquire language largely through imitation dates back to the work of Skinner, who was a researcher who very much believed in a rather simplistic reward model. Put very simply he believed that much of language acquisition came about through imitation and through reinforcement. So the child makes a sound; the adult interprets the sound as meaningful and praises the child; the child repeats the sound. Put crudely the model looks like this:

1 The child babbles and within the string of sounds comes something that sounds like 'mama'.
2 The mother thinks the child has learned to say the word for mother and kisses the child.
3 The praise – the positive reinforcement – makes the child say the word again, hoping for another kiss or (hug or banana).
4 The child has learned to say 'mama'.

Using language in order to communicate is a milestone in development. What is fascinating is that this remarkable intellectual feat, which usually takes place within the first year of life, occurs without anyone giving the child lessons. No one sets out to teach the child to talk. Rather, children begin to communicate with other beings through gesture, eye-pointing, expression, intonation and eventually through talk. In this social world children are surrounded by people who use talk in many, many different situations and use talk in order to communicate. The talk children encounter in their homes and communities is talk for real purposes and between people who want to share meaning. There are no tests to fail or trick questions to answer. So the human infant, working hard to understand communication, does so in the supportive company of people who want to communicate with him or her.

Quite how children achieve the remarkable feat of acquiring their first language in a very short time and without any explicit teaching is the subject of much debate. Noam Chomsky (1975), an American thinker and writer, was the first to suggest that language acquisition is genetically determined. He believed that the human infant is born pre-programmed to work out the rules of speech. If you think about it you will realise that speech – in any language – must be rule-governed if people are to be able to use it and be understood. In English, for example, there are rules about the order of words. We can say 'The dog jumped over the fence' but if we say 'The fence jumped over the dog' it makes no sense because a fence cannot jump. If we say 'The jumped fence the over dog' we are uttering a string of exactly the same words but in an order that prevents it from being meaningful. The same rule does not necessarily apply to other languages. In English we have rules about how we use verbs when we talk about the past tense. So we say 'we walked' and 'we talked': the rule being that we add 'ed' to the end of the verb. We have rules about how to talk about more than one object. So we talk about shoes and socks and pens and pencils. The rule here is that we add the letter 's' to the end of a noun to make that noun plural. You, as a fluent speaker of the language, will know that there are exceptions to the rules. We say 'went' instead of 'goed' and 'flew' instead of 'flied'; we talk of sheep instead of sheeps. Chomsky noticed that young children, having started out by saying things correctly through imitating what they have heard adults and fluent speakers say, move on to making mistakes by applying the rules to *all* situations. The way in which Chomsky described this was that the children were *over-generalising* the rules. He used this as evidence that children are brilliant thinkers, working out the patterns they hear to make up the rules and then, logically, applying them to all situations.

It was these errors that suggested to Chomsky that children must have something that allows them to use the patterns they hear to work out the rules. What he proposed was that the structure of language, by which he meant the rules that bind it together to make it meaningful, depends on what he called a *Language Acquisition Device* (LAD). You will remember that language has to be rule-bound and the rules known to all for it to be used for sharing meaning. The rules that bind language together are its grammar. The LAD had as its foundation what Chomsky called a '*universal grammar*' or a linguistic '*deep structure*' which he believed all human beings are born with. The LAD is programmed to recognise, in the surface structure of any natural language (i.e. the words and other features), how the deep structure will operate. So the surface features of the language which are particular to that language (to English or to Urdu or to Zulu, for example) allow it to be operated by the universal blueprint. This is what accounts for the fact that any human being is born capable of learning to communicate in any language. These are difficult ideas to comprehend and his is an extreme view.

For Chomsky children were seen as potentially competent users of language from birth. By competence Chomsky was talking about the underlying and unconscious knowledge of the rule system for generating language that they are born with. The errors, or the mistakes that children make, show us the efforts they are making to find the patterns in the particular language, to work out the rules and apply them. Here are some examples to make this clearer:

> 15-month-old Antonio points to the plastic farm animals he is playing with and labels them – 'cows, horses, sheep'.

Here you can see that this very young child is imitating the correct form of plurals he has heard the fluent speakers in his world use. He has not yet worked out the pattern that operates in English for making plurals. One might say that he is 'just copying'.

> Later, at the age of 3 Antonio points to the plastic sheep and labels them 'sheep**s**'.

Now the child has moved on from making a grammatically correct response to making an error or a mistake. Had Chomsky been presented with this specific example of a marked change in the child's use of language he would have said that initially Antonio had been paying attention to what he heard but, as part of paying attention, he gradually worked out that adults have a pattern for making plurals: they add an 's' at the end of the word. So the second example shows that the child has started to use the rule to form all plurals. He hasn't yet learned what we know: that there are often exceptions to the rules. The consequence is that he applies the rule to all situations. In the language of Chomsky he *over-generalises* the rule. No amount of correction at this stage will enable him to rectify his errors. It is only when he has discovered that there are rules and exceptions to rules that he will be able to use both forms. In other words, only with experience of listening to experienced others will he self-correct.

Steven Pinker (1994) is a linguist who was very influenced by the work of Chomsky and who went on to write about aspects of Chomsky's thinking in his book *The Language Instinct*. This is a very readable and chatty book, full of amusing games with language combined with some intricate explanations. The very title of the book, 'the language *instinct*', points to the view of language acquisition that he shared with Chomsky – that it was genetically determined. Pinker tells us that from Chomsky we learn two things:

1   That language cannot be merely a repertoire or a range of responses since everything anyone says or understands is a new or novel combination of words. When a child says 'The birds flied off' or 'I seed it and I feeled it and it's not a dog' each of these is a unique set of words, making meaning, but never before uttered by any human being. So the brain must hold a recipe or a programme or a blueprint that can build an infinite number of sentences out of a finite list of words. These are known as mental grammars.

2   That children develop these mental grammars which are very complex extremely rapidly and without formal teaching.

Jerome Bruner, another theorist, was influenced by the work of Chomsky and saw it as taking thinking about how children acquire language a leap forward from previous theories. He was very interested in language and particularly in talk. He did, however, notice a gap in Chomsky's theory and it is possible that you, too, might have noticed that Chomsky makes no reference to the role of other people in the child's learning of a first language. This meant that he ignored completely the roles of other people, which meant ignoring the importance of inter-action, as well as of culture and of context. For Bruner the development of language requires at least two people involved in exchange, communication and negotiation. The purpose of language is communication and it is through communication that meaning is made and shared and fine-tuned. So, building on Chomsky's LAD, Bruner proposed a more socio-cultural model which he called the Language Acquisition Support System (LASS). This he conceived of as a kind of adult scaffolding system. Children learn language through their interactions with others, who cue the children's responses and share meanings with them in particular contexts and within cultures. What emerges from this is the following:

-   Children acquire their first language through their interactions with significant others in the context of real life.
-   The people interacting with children provide models for them but also allow them to start and lead encounters.
-   Children pay close attention to what they hear and see around them and start to make attempts to communicate with others through eye-pointing, pointing, gesture, vocalising, intonation and any other means available to them.

- Imitation certainly plays a role in first-language learning as we see when young children repeat what they have heard fluent speakers say – so they produce plurals, for example, which break the grammatical rule in English of adding an 's' to the end of words.
- The errors that children make indicate that they must have come to the conclusion that there are patterns or rules governing the use of language and they then go through a phase of applying the rules they have worked out to all situations. This accounts for children making errors relating to plurals, for example.
- Children also make 'novel utterances' – which means that they say things that are entirely original and unique to them, saying things they can never have heard anyone else say.
- Language itself is rule-governed and it has to be if it is to be a system shared and used by whole communities of people. More than that, it is fluid and dynamic and ever-changing.

BECOMING A SIMULTANEOUS BILINGUAL

All the children you encounter will already have acquired or learned their first language. This means that they will have learned through their interactions with others within the context of their homes and communities, involved in the daily rituals of domestic life, and by paying close attention to all that happens to them. They will have listened to and imitated the sounds of the particular language, worked out the patterns and rules that apply to that language and then applied and over-applied them and made mistakes. They will have developed ways of communicating with others and will use language for different purposes and with different audiences. You may read this with irritation because it seems so obvious: all children will learn their first language with equal skill and concentration. The reason for mentioning what seems obvious is that many people tend to think that children who don't yet speak English have not yet learned anything. That is a dangerous and damaging myth.

Some of the children you encounter may appropriately be described as being bilingual and they are usually children who have learned or acquired more than one language from birth. These children have become bilinguals through the process of what is called *simultaneous bilingualism*. It is likely that for these children, within the immediate family are speakers of more than one language so that these children hear, from birth, the sounds of these languages and learn the patterns and rules that apply to them. It is thought that for these children the acquisition of two or more languages happens at the same time. Here are some small case studies to illustrate this.

Zeynep has learned both Turkish and English from birth. Her mum is Turkish and her dad English.

Christopher has learned both Greek and English from birth. Both of his parents are Greek Cypriots but his mum spent most of her life in England and insists on speaking and reading to him in English.

Dario and Cleo grew up in a family hearing both Italian and English from birth and German from soon after birth. Their mother spoke to them in English or Italian; their father in Italian only; and their grandparents, who came to live next door, used German in their presence.

Harry heard Yiddish, Russian and German spoken in his home. At the age of 5 his family moved to South Africa and he had to learn Afrikaans and English.

These children can all be described as having acquired their languages simultaneously and you can see from these brief and true case studies how different each case can be.

It will, perhaps, not surprise you to learn that there are those who argue that the presence of two languages can only confuse the child and for years it was believed that children experiencing simultaneous bilingualism were likely to be 'retarded'. Recent research (Meisel, 2004 and Genesee, 2003, for example) argues that babies appear to be biologically prepared and ready not only to acquire or learn two or more languages but also to remember and store these languages. To do this they have to be able to see the differences between their languages and to discriminate between them. Mehler *et al.* (1988) showed that infants can distinguish the sounds of their parents' native language from unfamiliar language sounds. It appears that when babies reach the babbling stage those exposed to two languages from birth will babble in their stronger language and will show some language-specific babbling features in each of their languages. Most fascinating is the evidence that bilingual children as young as 2 years old know which language to speak and to whom. The research of Deuchar and Quay (2001) showed that these very young bilinguals were able to choose which language to use with which person but also to match the language to the context. Cleo and Dario almost invariably talked to their father in Italian, asked their mother to read to them in English and demanded German songs and rhymes from their grandparents. Christopher asked me to read him a Greek story and when I said that I could not speak or read Greek he was astounded. Since his mother spoke both English and Greek he assumed her friend would also do so.

When very young bilingual children talk to strangers there is evidence from the work of Genesee *et al.* (1996) that they work out which language is spoken by a monolingual stranger and then use that language in their interactions with him or her. In the research Dutch/English bilingual 3-year-olds showed a willingness to use both languages (in other words, to code-switch) when in conversation with people they knew to be bilingual. We have encountered code-switching in a previous chapter and it is interesting that bilinguals may well continue to code-switch well into adulthood. Indeed, a colleague of mine, who is fully bilingual, always counts in French – even when counting occurs in the middle of something she is saying in English.

So we know that simultaneous bilinguals are able to differentiate between their two languages and even to make choices about which language to use with which people and in which context. This is a higher-order cognitive skill and it is worth remembering this.

Datta (2000) charts her own development as a multilingual child, growing up with her brothers and sisters in Nairobi, where she heard the sounds of many languages – kiSwahili, Punjabi and Gujarati, English and other European languages. She and her siblings spoke Bengali at home, and she used Punjabi as what she calls her 'friendship' language and Hindi and English as her school languages. She did not start school until the age of 7 and until then was taught, along with her siblings, by her mother, to read and write in Bengali and Hindi and English almost simultaneously. She adds:

> it was not an insurmountable task for my mother, nor were we prodigious children.

> (2000: 3)

and goes on to analyse what factors made this possible. She notes that all Indian languages have a common lexis (or vocabulary) and a set of grammatical rules which come from Sanskrit. In Bengali the alphabet has 40 consonants and 12 vowels: English, by comparison, has 21 consonants and 5 vowels but it is a non-phonetic language and there are 44 phonemes. Bengali, then, is a language where the phonic rules are followed and a competent speaker of the language can learn to read relatively easily. So the young Manjula learned to read in Bengali with ease. The transfer to Hindi, too, was relatively easy since the two languages share a common lexis and syntax although there are some differences in script, pronunciation and the use of the operative verb. Datta talks of there being '*a fluid interchange of knowledge, concepts and skills*' (2000: 4) between her three languages and says that this was what enabled her to become biliterate. Her learning to read in English was more complex and involved learning to say the alphabet, followed by a grapho-phonic approach to reading. The vital point here is that this learning took place once the child had already learned to read in two languages and was secure both about her own abilities and about the way in which her mother had taught her to read. Nonetheless her reading in English was simple decoding but she was neither excited not motivated to read in English. That was true until she read to her father in English when he brought to the text something extra. He embellished the text by telling his own stories, using words from these simple primers being by his daughter. It was this, the interaction with the text and the linking of it with experiences from her father's life, that brought reading in English alive for her. The implications of this are powerful. Reading, when it is for meaning and for pleasure and associated with pleasurable interactions, can be one of life's greatest pleasures.

It was thought, until recently, that simultaneous bilinguals initially operated just like monolinguals, using a single language system. In other words it was thought that bilingual children acquiring two languages from birth stored the words and grammars from their languages in one unitary system. Recent research by Genesee (2001), however, suggests that the languages of the bilingual child are stored as two separate language systems. These appear to develop autonomously, but are also interdependent. You already know that children who have two or more languages consciously or unconsciously make choices about which language to use where and with whom. These choices are influenced by the choices their parents made but sometimes children reject one of the languages for complex reasons. When Harry's family moved to South Africa his parents – who were poor and ill-educated – made the choice to speak to him only in Yiddish or English. The reasons for this were that their English was minimal but they believed that for him to succeed they all needed to speak only English. This is still the attitude of some families and parents – and even teachers – in this country today. The effect on Harry was that he lost every word of his first language, Russian, and could never regain it in later life.

This brings us to a point which is important for us all. There is, in all countries, a hierarchy of languages where some languages have high status and others little or no status. In this country English is regarded as supreme but speakers of European languages like French and Italian are regarded as 'fortunate' or 'clever' whereas speakers of Somali or Hindi are regarded as knowing nothing special.

In his first novel, Tash Aw, a young writer in London, writes a story set in what was then Malaya. In setting the scene for the dramatic events of the story he talks of the narrator's ancestors who came from the south of China – from Guangdong and Fujian provinces, where, he tells us, the people spoke two distinct languages. He says:

> This is important because your language determined your friends and enemies. People in our town speak mainly Hokkien, but there are number of Hakka speakers too . . . The literal translation of 'Hakka' is 'guest-people', descendants of tribes defeated in ancient battles and forced to live outside city walls. These Hakkas are considered by the Hokkiens and other Chinese here to be really very low class, with distinct criminal tendencies. No doubt they were responsible for the historical tension and bad feelings with the Hokkiens in these parts. Their one advantage, often used by them in exercising subterfuge and cunning, is the similarity of their language to Mandarin, the noble and stately language of the Imperial Court, which makes it easy for them to disguise their dubious lineage.
>
> (Tash Aw, *The Harmony Silk Factory*, 2005: 8)

This extract is full of snobbery and prejudice, but it highlights some salient features about how some socially aspiring people determinedly lose or change their language in order to be perceived differently. In this way they attempt to change their identity in order to play the particular roles in society they aspire to. If you consider this carefully you will realise that there are many people in your own society who try to change their language or dialect or accent in order to become more acceptable to others or more successful. We are back to seeing how language is intimately connected to power and how language, itself, can enhance or diminish status.

You may have encountered bilingual children who become the translators and interpreters for older members of the family. Harry and his siblings had to regularly accompany one or other of their parents to the doctor's surgery, the tax office, the school and other places where their limited English was of little use, but the children's fast-growing efficiency in the language allowed transactions to be completed. Baker (2006) re-tells an anecdote of a child not only translating for her father but reinterpreting – what Baker calls a cultural translation:

> The father said to his daughter, in Italian, 'Digli che e un imbecile!' which literally translates into 'Tell him he is an idiot'. The daughter's version of this to the shopkeeper was 'My father won't accept your offer.'
>
> (2006: 114)

BECOMING A SEQUENTIAL OR CONSECUTIVE BILINGUAL

In reality, most of the bilingual children you will encounter in your work will be those who have learned or are learning a second language after having already learned their first language. Some of these may well be children who are already bilingual but who are learning English as an additional language. These children will be learning or acquiring language through both formal and informal means, learning English through watching the television, playing with other children, on the streets, in nurseries and other settings or in classrooms and playgrounds in school. Baker (2006) tells us that many children become competent bilinguals through the process of simultaneous bilingualism but the track record of success for those becoming bilingual through subsequent or sequential bilingualism is less good. Despite years of 'foreign language' or 'second language' or English as a Second Language (ESL) teaching in both this country and the United States it appears that only a small proportion of children learning a second language through school become fully, functionally and fluently bilingual.

This is a concerning finding and one that affects all of us involved in the care and education of young children. If traditional ways of inducting young children into English are failing to produce fully bilingual adults, what is going wrong? Before suggesting answers it is worth noting that certain countries – notably the Netherlands, Sweden, Israel and Singapore – are far more successful at teaching newcomers the languages of the countries involved. We need to examine a number of factors which play a part in all of this.

There are a host of reasons why languages are taught in schools and as many reasons why children learn particular languages. Some of the reasons are personal and individual. Some people choose to learn a language because they want to know more about a particular culture or for work purposes or out of pure interest. Some have to learn a language in order to survive in a new country and culture. This applies particularly to the children with whom we work. They have been brought here and, in order to survive, communicate and succeed, must learn the language of the host culture. In doing this they start to play some very adult roles within their homes and communities because, as their proficiency in English increases, they become spokespeople for their families. The reasons for teaching a second language vary too and are often closely related to political ideology or economic necessity. During the 1980s the teaching of English within schools was based on a more respectful view of different languages and different cultures. Over the past two decades this has changed in response to changing conditions in the world and the perceptions of policy-makers regarding these. Think about the impact of 9/11 on all of us. If you are particularly interested in this you can read more about it in Baker (2006).

For us, the majority of children becoming bilingual with English as an additional language in our schools and settings are those who have come to live in this country with their parents. There are numerous reasons for coming to this country and those who come do so for a variety of reasons. There are a few people who come chasing particular jobs and planning to return home. They are often wealthy and well-educated people. It is likely that their first languages are those that are regarded as 'worth having'. There are many who come here as migrant workers, primarily to try to improve their standard of living. There are those who are fleeing desperate conditions of warfare or hunger or oppression or poverty at home and seek asylum and refuge here. Many of these may be well-educated and have to contend with doing menial work here rather than the things they were educated to do.

These are some of the people who are living in this country and they need to learn English. So the reasons for our teaching of English as an additional language and their learning of English as an additional language are to ensure that they become able to make relationships, learn to communicate with others, learn to read and write as well as speak and understand English and in these ways are more fully integrated into this society. But full integration should never mean the loss of culture, language and identity. So how we teach this subsequent language is important.

Li Wei (2000) has written powerfully about the experience of Chinese children in Britain. The Chinese are the third largest non-indigenous group in Britain and the majority of Chinese came here during the late 1950s and early 1960s. Today there is a large number of British-born Chinese and Wei identifies three distinct subgroups within the Chinese community. These are: (1) first-generation emigrants mainly from Hong Kong and south-east China; (2) sponsored emigrants, mainly kin to first-generation emigrants or with personal ties to others in this country; and (3) the British-born Chinese who are predominately under the age of 30. There is some previous research by Ng (1982) which illustrated some concern within the Chinese community that this third group was growing up with values which were not those of traditional China. The young people were said to lack respect for their culture and their language and were thought to be thoroughly anglicised. As a consequence of these findings numbers of out-of-school classes were set up in the Chinese communities to promote a knowledge of Chinese language and culture specifically within this community.

Wei's study took place in Newcastle upon Tyne, in a Chinese community school, and focused on examining the role of parents in their children's bilingual development. The findings of the study will not surprise you. In general Wei found that children of a similar age vary widely in terms of their ability to use their mother tongue and this variation is related to the language ability of their parents and also to the social network patterns both of the children themselves and of their parents. Those parents who were able to establish non-Chinese ties (meaning ties with people who are not Chinese) as part of their social worlds and had a better command of English were better able to maintain their mother tongue compared to those whose parents limited their relationships to immediate family and to those within their ethnic community. The British-born children who established peer ties with non-Chinese peers tended to improve their command of English but often at the expense of maintaining their first language.

SUMMARY

In this chapter we have looked at the fascinating and contentious views on how children acquire their first language – examining the complex ideas of Chomsky and those of his critics who feel that his analysis ignores the vital role of others in language acquisition. We then moved on to look at bilingual children who learn more than one language at the same time and those who acquire another language or languages after having learned their first language.

GLOSSARY

Blueprint	A plan of something.
Code-switching	Changing languages in the same sentence or utterance.
Communicative	To do with communication and the sharing of meaning.
Cultural translations	Interpreting more than just the words and thinking about the impact they might have on the listener.
Decoding	To sound out the words and read them sometimes accurately but not for meaning.
Genetically determined	Something that is decided by genes.
Imitation	Copying
Lexis	Vocabulary
Linguistic symbols	Letters or ideograms building up into words.
Mental grammars	The rules governing language that seem to be held in the mind.

Novel utterance	Something that has never before been said; it is a term used to explain what we all do when we use language creatively.
Over-generalising	A term used by Chomsky to describe what children do when they always apply a rule they have devised and what happens before they realise that there are exceptions to the rules.
Reinforcement	This means responding to something in a way which allows the action either to be repeated or causes it to be abandoned. Positive reinforcement (often seen as praise or reward) is aimed at causing an observed response to be repeated. Negative reinforcement (often seen as punishment) is aimed at causing an observed response not to be repeated.
Rule-bound	Something which is held together by rules and which would not work without the rules. In language the rules (which means the grammar) are what enable people to communicate with one another and to make and share meaning.
Sequential bilingualism	The acquisition of a language after the acquisition of the first language; sometimes called sequential bilingualism or consecutive bilingualism.
Simultaneous bilingualism	The acquisition of more than one language from birth.
Sociocultural	A theory or an action that takes account of the roles of others and of customs and beliefs and practices of groups of others.
Symbolic acts	A symbol is a sign and in our societies language itself is symbolic. In other words a word, spoken or written, represents or stands for something that may not be present. So speaking and reading and writing are symbolic acts. An understanding of the symbolic nature of language is important in learning and comes about largely through children playing with objects and pretending that one thing represents another.
Syntax	Grammar – or the rules binding a language.

Chapter 5

Issues in effective teaching 1: mother-tongue support in learning

In this chapter we look at what is currently thought about why it is important for children to retain their first language and have access to it for learning.

We look at some examples of ways of doing this, including examining immersion programmes, heritage language programmes, and the role of bilingual adults in learning.

We look, too, at the use of resources including dual-language books and audio materials.

MAINTAINING THE USE OF FIRST LANGUAGE IN SCHOOLS OR SETTINGS

You are invited to read the two case studies below and in each case to imagine what it feels like to be the child. In each of the case studies the child is a 5-year-old boy.

Abdul was brought into the reception class by his dad who spoke almost no English. A neighbour accompanied them and explained that they had arrived from a village in Bangladesh the night before and that Abdul (who he believed was 5 years old) had never been out of the village before, had never been to school and had, of course, no English. At the school there were no Sylheti-speaking adults or children, so no one to help the terrified little boy understand what was happening. The teacher welcomed him into the class and got another child who was a newcomer and who had little or no English to sit beside him. This child, unfortunately, was not a Sylheti speaker but an Urdu speaker, which was of little help to Abdul.

Abdi arrived from Somalia with his family and after a week his mother brought him into the school to register him for the reception class. There were several other Somali families at the school and the head-teacher invited one of these to attend the meeting to interpret for the family. Through the interpreter she explained to the mother that one of the teaching assistants was a Somali speaker and the head would ensure that this woman would be present on Abdi's first morning to ease his transition into school. On his first day Ms Ekboni spoke to him quietly in Somali and showed him the things in the room, including some books in Somali and English. She showed him where the toilets were, explained about playing outside in the special playground and introduced him to other children, one of whom, a confident monolingual English speaker, offered to 'look after him'. Ms Ekboni ensured that she returned at dinner time to help him with what is sometimes a difficult situation.

It seems glaringly obvious that Abdi has had an easier start to his school career than Abdul. Being helped to understand what is happening in a completely new environment must facilitate any child's adjustment and although we know how adaptable most children are it is something that is worth considering carefully for all new children. Clearly with the range of languages spoken by newcomers to our schools and settings we are not able to provide interpreters and translators for all, but the principle remains.

Baker (2006) tells us that schools and nurseries are complex organisa-tions where there are many people playing many roles throughout the day; where there are rules and conventions, expectations and demands, rewards and punishments, and needs and concerns. Clearly it is not possible for any one institution to meet the needs and expectations of all pupils and their parents. But when we think what makes a class or a setting effective for bilingual children, it seems obvious that the ethos is important. We are thinking here about what messages newcomers to the class or setting get from the attitudes of the adults and children, the displays on the walls, the resources, the teaching styles, the groupings and so on. Looking less superficially we are interested also in the attitude of the school or nursery or setting to the use of mother tongue/first language per se. In essence we are asking if there is evidence that the school or setting recognises the incontrovertible fact that learning is most successful where the learner has access to using this first language within the class or setting. So this is a chapter about *maintaining and promoting first-language development*.

In reality it is not possible for every child in this country to actually learn in school or setting through her or his mother tongue. Learning, however, takes place not only in the school or setting, but also in the home, in the community and often in community schools, specifically set up for the purposes of maintaining home languages and cultures. And whilst no one might expect each school or setting to actually teach the children through their first languages there are strategies for indicating to parents and families and children themselves that the maintenance of the mother tongue is essential both for the child's learning and for the child's social development.

UNESCO (1953) in a report called *The Use of Vernacular Languages in Education* argued that learning through the child's mother tongue ensured that children could build on what they already knew. More than 50 years ago this document managed to cite examples of countries throughout the world where teaching in mother tongue took place in the early years with the host language gradually being taught to the children on entry to school and even more gradually taking over as the language of instruction. In the examples cited it is interesting to note that children were not only taught *in* their first language but also taught their first language. This meant that children learned not only vocabulary but also the rules of language, its signs and symbols and its social significance. The authors of the report argued that this allowed (1) sociological benefits in that the child could remain close to his or her family and local community and (2) educational benefits because learning across the curriculum was more effective in a known language. Such learning, they argued, also eased the often traumatic move from home to school. It seems certain that the use of mother tongue in the early years should be promoted as much as possible because it is the language the child understands best. There is some evidence to show that this goes way beyond the early years and applies to some concepts that are well understood in this first language but extremely difficult to grasp in another language.

The Centre for Applied Linguistics (2001) tells us that supporting mother-tongue use builds self-esteem and actually helps the learning of a second language.

> When the mother tongue is not used, they [the children] are made to feel backward, inferior, and stupid. This can have long term effects.
> (Centre for Applied Linguistics, 2001: 19)

In the UK it is apparent that first-language acquisition and use are promoted primarily through the system of complementary schools provided by communities and offered after school times or at weekends. These are not part of the state education system. Mother-tongue support in schools and settings is limited, sometimes dependent on where the school is situated and what its approach to languages is. The mother tongue is supported mainly through encouraging children to speak and use their first languages in and out of class and through employing speakers of these languages as teachers or nursery nurses or teaching/support assistants. The provision of resources in the languages of the children may be helpful in at least showing recognition of and respect for linguistic diversity.

Teaching styles may also impact on the retention of first language. Where schools adopt the so-called *'banking'* or *'transmission'* approach to teaching – i.e. where knowledge is passed on by the person with power (the teacher) to those without power (the students) – there is little opportunity for learners to use their own experience and knowledge to any effect. In schools where a different approach is used there is more likelihood of learners using their first language when they feel the need to understand and make sense of their learning. This style of pedagogy is known as *dialogic teaching* or *'transformative pedagogy'* (Cummins, 2000). Here bilingual learners and monolingual learners are able to contribute to a more open and cooperative approach to knowledge *building* rather than knowledge transmission. What happens is more of a dialogue between teacher and learner with both contributing, both drawing on their experience and both negotiating and making meaning.

Let us look at an example of such teaching. It, again, comes from the work of Kenner (2004b). In the introductory chapter Kenner described some of the things that happened in the classrooms of the children in her study. She reminded us that, although we have a National Curriculum and the strategies, teachers and practitioners are able to interpret these individually and flexibly. The bilingual children in Kenner's study attended a range of schools which were making attempts to demonstrate their awareness of how much learning takes place in the home and in the community. One of the things attempted in the schools in the study was to adopt teaching styles which were based on a dialogue with the children.

> One of the teachers was working on story-writing and discussed with the whole class things like how to incorporate everyday events into narratives and stories and then to see how these narratives could be made more exciting and dramatic by the introduction of 'something unusual'. Sadhana, in this class, wrote a story about going to the park (for her this was an everyday event) where she saw her grandmother from Ecuador (for her the unusual and dreamed-of event).

> In Brian's class they were following a topic on light and dark. The teacher asked the children to think about how they would describe their own house to someone with visual difficulties. The children had to explain how to get from one room to another. To get a feeling for what it would be like to be unable to see the children were asked to draw their house with their eyes closed.

Neither of these is a startling example, but they illustrate ways of offering children activities which will allow them to build on their out-of-school/ setting experience. What is important here is that instead of the teacher having control and telling the children what to do, the teacher (or teaching assistant or nursery nurse) engages in a dialogue with the children, asking them to give their thoughts and ideas. This allows the children to draw on what they already know and have already experienced and also to introduce the things that are of interest to them. Early years practitioners will be more familiar with this sort of approach than educators in Key Stage 1 and beyond.

Here are some ways of learning more about learning at home, at complementary school and in the community.

▷ Ask carefully phrased questions to show children that you are interested in the languages used in their homes and families. You can ask about favourite TV programmes in other languages, stories heard, books read and so on.

▶ Ask children to bring in written materials from home – newspapers, magazines, calendars, videos. This is to show your interest in the scripts, alphabets and ideograms used and could be part of a project on writing. Ask all the children to look for examples of writing in other languages in the environment.

▶ Involve all the children in talking about languages they know about. This can come from holidays, relatives, friends, neighbours, shops. Monolinguals may surprise you!

▶ Talk to the parents about why knowledge about different languages is important for all children living in this multilingual world.

▶ Create a photo display of the children showing the languages they are learning out of school through complementary schools. You need to do this sensitively and ensure that there are children who are learning other languages out of school/ setting.

▶ You may want to celebrate festivities of the children in the school or setting (Eid, Chinese New Year and so on), but take care not to let this be tokenist. Involve local community leaders and the teachers in the community schools, if possible.

(With thanks to Kenner, 2004b)

HERITAGE LANGUAGE SCHOOLS AND COMPLEMENTARY SCHOOLS

You may find that you are working in a school or setting which has a specific policy to actually teach entirely or partly through more than one language, where one of these is the first language of some of the children. It is likely that, where this is the case, your 'teaching' of the first language will involve using both languages to teach the curriculum. This is the case in Wales, where conscious efforts are being made for the minority language (Welsh) to be made increasingly available in what were previously English domains – in education, on television and through pop music.

Programmes such as these can be defined as those that are trying to ensure that minority languages do not die out or remain as low-status languages in society. In the USA and some other places they are termed '*heritage language*' schools. In this country and in Australia these are out-of-school rather than in-school programmes. The features of heritage language programmes are as follows.

- Parents may have the choice of sending their children to these schools or to mainstream schools.
- The minority language will be used for about 50% of the curriculum time. There is often the tendency to teach science and technology through the majority language.
- Where the minority language is used for the majority of classroom time the justification is that children will easily transfer ideas, concepts, skills and knowledge into the majority language.
- A minority language is thought to be easy to lose whilst a majority language is easy to gain since children are bathed in this in the society in which they live.
- The majority of these schools are primary schools, although in Wales heritage language schools are available until the end of secondary education and in South Africa the boast is that students can select any of the 11 official languages in which to study right up to the end of their university courses.

IMMERSION PROGRAMMES

Another approach to bilingualism and to the promotion and maintenance of first language is immersion education and the most famous example of this comes from Canada. This started as an educational experiment in the 1960s when, it is said, a group of English-speaking, middle-class parents persuaded their school district to set up an experimental kindergarten for 26 children to teach them to speak, read and write in French whilst reaching what were regarded as 'normal' standards of achievement in English, and also to appreciate the customs and traditions of French-speaking Canadians. We could describe this as aiming to make the children both bilingual and bicultural. Do remember, as you read this, that French and English are both high-status languages and one needs to question whether the same might have been true if the two languages had been English and Inuit.

Immersion programmes now operate in many countries of the world and differ in terms of the ages at which children start in these programmes and in the amount of time spent in immersion. There is much you can read about these programmes if they are of particular interest to you. They have been extensively researched and continue to be developed in more and more countries. In Finland, for example, they were not started in response to parent requests, but rather through a political analysis of the difficulties that had been faced by many Finnish children of migrant workers having to be educated in Sweden. Now programmes in Finland include not only the original languages of Swedish and Finnish, but also English and German. Hopefully you remember the very moving story of young Antti and what happened to him when he went to school in Sweden. Now, in Finland – the country he left – schools are producing multilingual students and also providing high-quality teacher education programmes to assist new teachers to cope with immersion programmes.

In the UK there are few, if any, immersion programmes and few state-provided heritage language schools. Rather there are monolingual schools, some of which make heroic efforts to promote and retain first-language use and many community schools where first-language use is taught and maintained. Sadly, the truth seems to be that mainstream schools, in general, make few efforts to know what takes place in these community schools and to integrate the learning that takes place in both. This offers exciting opportunities for research and development, building on the work of people like Kenner and Gregory and Drury and Sneddon, some of whose work you have already encountered and some of whom you will meet in the chapters that follow.

THE ROLE OF BILINGUAL ADULTS

You may be bilingual and working with bilingual children, or you may work alongside other adults who speak the languages of the children. You will know how invaluable such support is. Cunningham (2000) cites the example of Whetley First School in Bradford, which employed bilingual teachers and teaching assistants, not as an accident (according to the headteacher) but as part of an appointment policy and because they believed that bilingual staff play a vital role in keeping children in touch with their world. In this school bilingual staff are paired with monolingual staff, wherever possible. So in maths, for instance, a monolingual adult will offer an instruction or an example or an explanation in English, immediately followed by the bilingual adult saying it in Punjabi, for example. There is considerable code-switching in this way and, in addition to this, the school has used transliteration of poems and rhymes and songs so that all those in the school can chant or say or sing them. Here is what Yasmin Ali says:

> [The previously monolingual teacher] can now sing 'Heads, Knees and Toes' in Urdu so fast and fluently I have trouble keeping up with her! She'll sing 'The Wheels on the Bus', one verse will be in English, the next in Punjabi and the children don't bat an eyelid.
>
> (Datta, 2000: 197)

Datta (2000) tells us of the progress of Nadia, a young Sylheti-speaking child attending an inner city school in London, a school where the majority of children were Sylheti speakers with roots in Bangladesh. In her classroom there were two support teachers, a Bengali-speaking English as an Additional Language (EAL) teacher and a mother-tongue teacher working alongside the class teacher three mornings a week. The mother-tongue teacher displayed a lot of code-switching and there was a good deal of team teaching. In fact, the classroom seemed to be characterised by a good deal of repetition as when the EAL teacher taught in English but repeated significant things in Bengali. This '*bilingual repetition*' is regarded by Gumperz (1982) as important in helping bilingual learners to internalise learning.

Ross (2000) tells us about how Mohsen, an Urdu speaker, progressed in his early years in school. She notes:

> A very important support for Mohsen was the opportunity he had to work with a member of the staff who could speak Urdu. In these sessions he had the opportunity to understand so much more, and to express much more fluently what he had done, seen and felt, what he wanted to find out or explore next, what might happen in a story . . . the support offered in his classroom provided a framework within which children who were 'silent' for longer could become members of the classroom community and share in the learning.
>
> (2000: 43)

RESOURCING TO SUPPORT RETENTION OF THE MOTHER TONGUE

One of the assertions made at the start of this chapter was that the maintenance and promotion of first language would do much to help bilingual children build their self-esteem, and to learn their second or additional language more confidently, and would allow them to develop socially. Any class or setting which seeks to achieve this needs to address the issue of resources.

Classes and settings should ensure that children coming into them will find *images of children like themselves*, coming from homes like theirs, and encounter the scripts and alphabets and sounds of their languages. There are many suppliers of books and posters, CD ROMs and other resources and one of the best-known supplies of these is Mantra. You may want to read what they say on their website (*www.mantralingua.com*).

The products connect with and transcend national differences in a way that is respectful and appreciative of local cultures. The name, MantraLingua, is an amalgam between the Sanskrit and Latin, but Mantra also covers the Far Eastern and the African continents.

MantraLingua is about connecting languages for children. With increased mobility of populations across the globe, e.g. Brazilians in Japan, Malis in Sweden, Indians in Gambia, MantraLingua has developed a set of values that stems from a desire to retain distinctness and yet encourage integration of new communities in various societies.

An outline of MantraLingua's values are as follows:

- To celebrate the cultural and linguistic nature of society and to establish a culture of tolerance and awareness in young people, both from the host and the new communities.
- To provide resources for ethnic minority groups with strong central characters and community settings, to consequently help in building the child's self-esteem and social interaction.
- To share across cultures the children's books that are special – taking best-selling well-known books and publishing them in as many languages as is economically feasible.

- To provide teachers and librarians with creative resource materials which are inclusive of all the community and are not dominated by one single culture.
- To strive for innovation and creativity in learning methods, promoting the values of bilingualism not only to enhance language skills but also in the learning of the major national language.
- To increase the awareness of the diversity of cultures and the enriching prospects for more cross-cultural activities and resources. Together these will make for a more global understanding of the nature and nuances of peoples from different countries or communities.

You will be able to find dual-text books published by well-known publishers like Walker Books and also by less well-known publishers like Milet Publications. Amazon stocks a fairly wide range of books as does Letterbox Library. The suppliers your school or setting uses will offer their own lists. Ideally you should match the books you select to the languages in your group or class although you may want to have other languages for particular reasons. Do remember that the creation of dual-text books is not without difficulties, particularly where directionality of text is an issue. You will find much of interest on www. nel.ac.uk/education/research/duallanguagebooks/.

Some *schools make their own dual-text or dual-language books* by asking the children to choose their favourite books and then asking the local translation unit or a parent or other adult speaker of a language other than English to translate the text. The versions created may be strange and not as attractive as published versions, but getting the children to illustrate them and involving the staff in sticking the translations under the text are useful learning experiences. Many years ago this was a project at a Hackney infants school and it was a salutary experience to have an older child or a parent come into the school to explain that the teachers had pasted the translated text under the English text upside down! Similarly, *making a library of dual-text books plus story props (cutout or felt models or small world toys of the characters in the story) plus taped versions of the story in English and other languages* offers wonderful opportunities for children to teach and learn from one another.

Story props and puppets can both be used for a range of purposes. They can be used to draw children with little English into the meaning of stories and can be placed alongside the book, to allow children to retell or re-create the stories for themselves. They can be used to find reasons for children to talk – either in their mother tongue or in English – for example, by saying that 'Teddy [for instance] was asleep and missed the story. Can you tell it to him/her?' They can be used to provide an audience for writing – sending invitations, thank-you letters, lists and so on.

SUMMARY

In this chapter we have looked at ways of promoting the use of mother tongue by children in schools and settings in order to benefit socially and cognitively. We have seen how heritage language programmes, where education is offered in more than one language, can benefit children. We have also looked at what can be done in the very complex situations to be found in many urban schools where tens of different languages may be spoken. There is a considerable body of research to show how effective some of the strong forms of bilingual education, like those offered in heritage language programmes, are. Despite this – and probably for political and economic reasons – such programmes remain rare and in this country are almost exclusively offered through community or complementary schools. The best we can do is to pay attention to the ethos of the school or setting, ensuring that respect for languages and cultures is prominent and overt and that children are never told to lose their first languages.

GLOSSARY

Banking style of education	This is where the teacher holds the information and passes it on to the learner. Useful metaphors are of the child as a blank slate or an empty vessel.
Bicultural	Offering or 'owning' more than one culture.
Bilingual repetition	The repetition of phrases in more than one language to aid recall.
Community school	The preferred term used for schools where heritage language teaching takes place.

Complementary schools	Examples of community schools, but offered not by the state but by communities, out of school hours, and committed to facilitating the learning of first language and of the culture of the group.
Dialogue	Where an exchange takes place in which all parties have views and are invited to share them.
Dual-language books	Books where two languages are presented alongside one another.
First language	Also called mother tongue, or L1, and the first language learned by the child, usually in the home.
Heritage language	A term favoured in the USA to describe the languages of minority groups. The term community languages is preferred in the UK.
Immersion	A system of bilingual education where children learning a second language are immersed in it and learn all their subjects in that language.
Internalise	To become very familiar with something so that it is easily recalled.
Tokenist	When something is done in order to create an impression rather than because much thought has gone into it. It is often used to describe the approach of some schools and settings to religions, for example, where celebrating Eid and Diwali is considered enough.
Transformative pedagogy	Synonymous with dialogic education and the opposite of banking education.
Transliteration	The rendering of another language using the letters and sounds of English, for example.

Chapter 6

Issues in effective teaching 2: learning a second language 💡

In this chapter we briefly examine the history of teaching English to children who already have a first language or languages.

We examine and critique a number of approaches currently being used to teach English as an additional language.

We take a look at useful resources for the teaching of English as an additional language.

The vast majority of bilingual children learn or acquire their second language once they start school or setting. For the majority of the bilingual children that we encounter this second language is English. These children learn English through events away from the home, but also through events at home. They hear English in the streets, at the clinic, in the shops and, most potently, on television, on their computers and on their electronic toys. At school or setting they hear English in the classroom and playground and the need to learn to communicate is pressing. They are highly motivated to learn to understand and to speak English in order to do so.

When migrant workers and refugees first came to this country, once there was a system of state education in place their children simply went to the monolingual English schools and were expected to sink or swim. You will remember this submersion model from an earlier chapter. If there were educational imperatives underlying this approach they certainly included a belief in cultural assimilation. Put simply, the idea was 'people who choose to come here should become like us' and this meant paying no heed to the languages and cultures which the children and their families brought with them. The effects on children have been documented over decades and it is clear from the examples below how damaging this approach can be:

> Inuit children were airlifted from their kinship-based communities into large, impersonal boarding schools in Canada. This resulted in more than the initial trauma of separation. The children became disobedient and disrespectful to their communities when they returned home in the holidays. They dissociated themselves from their parents and families and looked down on them and on their culture.

> In the USA the teachers in the schools for Navajo children were mainly white English speakers who came from outside of the reservations where the children lived. These teachers spoke no Navajo and could not communicate easily with either children or parents. The style of learning was based on learning by doing whereas traditional Navajo culture emphasised learning through long observation, almost an apprenticeship. Children grew up in fear of being mocked, estranged from their families and stigmatised at school.

> (Drawn from Grosjean, 1982)

However, once an awareness grew that ignoring the languages and cultures of the children was potentially damaging, thought was given to how to teach English as an additional language and one development was that of the 'withdrawal group'. You may well be familiar with this, perhaps from your own experience or that of your children. Here, children with little or no English, were taken out of the mainstream class on a regular basis and placed with a teacher, sometimes specially trained as a teacher of English as an additional (or second or foreign, depending on when and where this happened) language. What went on within these groups varied, of course, but here is an example of some experiences of those who endured them.

> Every day during story time, for a whole year, I had to go out of the class with all the other children in my year, for an English lesson. The teacher was an English speaker. We were, none of us, English speakers nor did we share a language. As I remember there were Vietnamese children, children from Pakistan and Bangladesh, from Nigeria and

Taiwan. The teacher insisted that we did not speak at all, except in response to her. Every day she would hold up a picture – a cup or an apple or a knife – say a word and makes us repeat, as a complete sentence 'This is a cup (or apple or knife)'. We had to wait for her to say, in a sing-song voice 'What is this?' and then, like a conductor, she would give us the signal to respond. I learned no English at all in her class. I learned my English on the street and in the playground. We all hated that group. We hated not being part of the class, hated missing story time, hated not being able to talk or be understood and hated, most of all, learning something that could not be called language!

(Personal communication, 2001)

For a brief time ideology in the UK changed as there was a growing recognition that bilingualism brought with it considerable cognitive advantages and that ignoring the languages and cultures of children in a multicultural world brought about alienation and discrimination.

This resulted in the flowering of some developments relating to the teaching of English to speakers of other languages, some of which are listed below. They are useful things for you to consider.

1   *Keeping speakers of languages other than English in the mainstream classroom at all times in order for them to have models of fluent use of English from their peers and in order not to stigmatise them.* This does not mean that these children should not receive special individual attention, where necessary, and this is best provided through *appointing speakers of the languages of the children* as teachers, teaching assistants, nursery nurses or other support workers. Their role is to mediate and to support the children in their learning. Ideally these people also need specialist training in order to understand current ideas on teaching and learning.

2   Ensuring that there is plenty of *contextual support for the language* being used, through body language, gesture, acting and facial expression. Schools and settings can share their knowledge and expertise by ensuring that those working in them have opportunities to observe successful teachers using these strategies in classes and settings.

3   *Knowing where the child has come from*, what the child knows and can do, and what the child has experienced, in order to use

77

these as the starting point of all teaching. The aim is to connect the unknown to the known, to build on prior learning and experience, which those reading this who are early years workers will recognise as a key principle of early learning.

4 *Extensive use of visual material* through the use of pictures and videos and other things to make sure that children can access the meaning. The technical term for this is 'comprehensible input'. Baker (2006) advises us that effective classrooms are where students and teachers are negotiating meaning, taking care that mutual understanding has been achieved. The learner has understood the teacher and the teacher has understood the learner.

5 *Using real life experiences or lifelike experiences or what are often called 'meaningful contexts'* (shopping and cooking and planting and so on) and concrete objects to ensure that meaning is shared

6 Recognising that learning is always valued in cultures but *ways of learning differ*. Learning through play or hands-on experience is much valued in early years education in this country but other styles of learning are much valued in other cultures. One of these is what Rogoff (1990) calls *apprenticeship* or *'guided participation'* where the learner is alongside a fluent or experienced person, watching, talking and listening.

7 Using a *curriculum bathed in language* (in this case English) so that new learners of English are constantly immersed in the language used by adults and children for real purposes. MacIntyre *et al.* (2001) tell us that willingness to communicate is enhanced when there are authentic uses for the language. This means language used for genuine exchanges as when children give their responses to situations or problems or questions and these are treated as part of a real and purposeful exchange. This is a long way from the example of the child learning English by having to repeat a set sentence as a chant.

8 *An emphasis on activities first involving speaking and listening*: this involves a recognition that new learners of a language often go through a *'silent period'* where they listen intently and learn the sounds and patterns of the new language. These children should be invited to speak in their first language to one

another or, if there is no one to share their first language, to remain silent for as long as they need to.

9   Educators need to have *high expectations for all pupils,* including those who have English as an additional language. This means that those working with these pupils need to recognise and respect their prior learning and experience – particularly that of having already learned their first language – and they need to expect the pupils to build on this linguistic knowledge and experience. Too often teachers and others expect children who are refugees or children of asylum seekers or migrant workers to be 'at risk', in some way. It is important, too, for educators to convey their high expectations to the children themselves and to their parents and carers.

10 Parents need to be involved as much as they can in a *genuine partnership* with the school or setting and their views need to be asked for and listened to. What the school or setting is trying to do needs to be communicated to parents and often this will involve using speakers of the languages of the parents to act as interpreters or translators. Keeping in touch with parents throughout the child's education is important.

Here are some small case studies for you to consider:

Minh Duc from Vietnam spent his first three months in his English school, totally silent. There were no other Vietnamese speakers in the school. The school operated a system of everyday book-sharing (prior to the introduction of the National Curriculum and the strategies) and the little boy would sit on the carpet and sort out the books in the boxes according to size and shape. This apparently random behaviour at first worried the teachers in the class, but they consulted advisory teachers who told them to be patient and watch and wait. They explained about the silent period. Both the educators in the room noticed that as time passed Minh Duc continued to sort the books but each day he moved his pile closer to the teacher who was sitting on a chair reading with one child after another. As soon as the child who had been reading had finished and put the book back in one of the boxes Minh Duc got up and took the book that had been read and pored over the pictures. After three months he

79

began to speak in English. Today he is studying for a Master's degree in Anthropology.

Maggie Ross (2000) tells us about Mohsen's experiences when he started school at the age of 4½, not yet speaking English but fluent in Urdu. He had some understanding of English and of the routines of school through his older brother. But once inside the classroom everything was new to him – and potentially scary. But Mohsen was fortunate because the teachers in his school had thought carefully about what they could do to make the classroom understandable. Routines were consistent but not rigid. Adults gave new children time to ease in and used photographs of activities to assist in this. So there were pictures of children washing their hands, lining up for dinner and out in the playground. Photographs were also used in resource areas throughout the room. At group times when children talked about what they wanted to do next photographs were invaluable. Mohsen could point to what he wanted to do and did not need to speak. Story sessions and singing were regarded as vitally important for language learning and songs and stories with repeated phrases of patterns were carefully selected. So Mohsen rapidly acquired a basic vocabulary of single words and he used gesture and pointing and intonation to enhance his communicative attempts. By the end of his first term he was able to use phrases like 'My mum say take this book home'. This was not achieved by magic but largely because in the class there was a member of staff who could speak Urdu and mediate for him. If you go back to the previous chapter you will be able to read, again, about how this adult helped his learning to take off. His silent period was comparatively brief but the teaching style, the classroom practice and the ethos in this class helped children who needed a much longer silent period emerge as fluent speakers of English.

Howell (cited in Cunningham, 2000) tells us about Stewart Hedlam Primary School and about how they act on their awareness of the fact that children need constant examples of teachers or other adults modelling talk to provide contextual and linguistic support for those children who are working on tasks which are cognitively challenging. This is a principle developed and explained by Cummins (1996). The policy of the school is to ensure that children are engaged in practically doing things and whilst they are doing this having the opportunity to discuss what they are doing, to ask questions and have these answered and to be helped to make connections. This example highlights several of the principles outlined above.

RESOURCES AND STRATEGIES FOR TEACHING CHILDREN WHO HAVE ENGLISH AS AN ADDITIONAL LANGUAGE

Music, songs, rhymes and nursery rhymes

Datta (2000) tells us that children respond to what she calls the 'rhythmic grouping' of the sounds in poetry and rhyme and that they seem to learn these easily and chant them. For children learning English as an additional language the opportunity to memorise and say these songs and poems and rhymes provides a sound foundation for building up their fluency in a new language. To do this there are several things practitioners can do:

1 *Start to build up a collection of songs and rhymes in English* and use frequent opportunities to sing these. Children can join in and become familiar with hearing and making the sounds of English which may be unfamiliar to them.
2 *Nursery rhymes*, for younger children, are a useful resource and making these into Big Books during shared reading or writing sessions offers the opportunity for repetition in a meaningful context.

The power of stories

Practitioners can offer children models of English in different forms through the books that they provide for children to look at and read for themselves (or retell in the case of younger children) and in terms of the books they read aloud each day. What is chosen should be of high quality in terms of the language used, the quality of the story and illustrations and the links they offer to the lives of the children. So primers with simple sentences on each page will not suffice. Practitioners will look for books which have rhymes or alliteration; using repeated phrases which invite the reader to join in (for example, 'Oh no!'

said Mr Bear, 'I can't stand this!') and where, in the story, something happens. Predicting what will happen next is a vital part of becoming a reader and a writer and well-written stories make children want to know what will happen next. There are many, many high-quality picture and story books available through any good bookshop. Look online to find a children's bookshop in your area or read the book reviews in quality newspapers or the educational press. Go to the local library and see what they have there. To make stories accessible to children with little or no English there are things you can do:

1 *Ensure that you have an excellent collection of picture and story books and read often to children individually, in small groups and in pairs.*
2 *Make looking at stories and retelling stories an integral part of your day.*
3 *Provide story props* (cut-out and laminated or felt characters or objects from the stories) which can be used on a felt board or a magnetic board to help the children get at the meaning.
4 *Use puppets to be the audience for the children's retelling of stories or rhymes* or to act out the stories and rhymes. Here is an account of what one bilingual support teacher said about the role of puppets in her work:

> I noticed that Shahanara was inattentive during the reading of a group story so left the book out for her to look at after the session and she seemed interested. The next day I brought in a puppet and asked Shahanara if she could tell him the story (it was *The Tiger Who Came to Tea*) because he had been absent the day before. She took the book and the puppet into one of the quiet corners and I could hear her little voice, piping away in a mixture of English and Sylheti. Later she brought him to me and said 'He likes to go to a café too' – which showed me that she had understood the story and could find a way of telling me about the puppet's reaction in English.
>
> (Personal communication, 2004)

5 *Make story packs of book plus taped or CD version* so children can listen to the story whilst they turn the pages and see the words and the pictures.

Sonay and Amy were best friends. They would often choose to listen to taped stories and it was fascinating watching them listen to a known story first in English and then in Turkish, each time tracking the words in the dual-text book. A fine example of children teaching and learning from one another.

6 *Make story packs of book plus props* so children can play with these whenever they have the urge to re-tell or make up a story.

7 *Use 'Talking Books'* if you think it appropriate. They offer moving pictures to create text and understanding. They have 'pages' and children can mimic what they would do with a real book in terms of finding the cover, turning the pages, following the lines of text and so on. These should be used as additional to story reading and not instead of it.

Collaborative games

Games that children can play together are very useful for encouraging communication around something shared and where the meaning is embedded in the context of the game. Collaborative games offer opportunities for children from as young as 4 to those designed for young adolescents. Here is an example to illustrate this:

Young children playing a game based on the book 'Each, Peach, Pear, Plum'. It is a board game with a track and the children have to try and collect nursery rhyme or fairy-tale characters and they do this by landing on rhyming words. So if they land on 'cellar' they can collect Cinderella and if they land on 'hill' they can collect Jill (and her partner Jack, of course). There is a dice and the possibility to decide on and vary the rules.

(Drawn from Datta, 2000)

You can buy many games but you can also make them for yourself and they can be number games or turn-taking games which provide the context for the children to use English as they play.

Book-making

Make book-making an essential feature of your class. These may be books you make for the younger children or books the children make for themselves or for their friends or family. The use of digital cameras and computers makes it possible for the books to look attractive and children can work collaboratively as they make up and record stories or record information.

In one school workshops were held for parents who wanted to come and learn to make books for their young children. The parents were invited to write simple stories, often using a series of repeated patterns of language – e.g. 'Oh, no!' said . . . 'I can't stand this' (based on the story of 'Peace at Last'). The teacher running the workshop used, as an example, a tiny book made with her reception class and called 'What a Class'. Here in Figure 6 is what the book looked like.

Figure 6

Parents were free to write in any language and could illustrate the books themselves or invite their children to do it for them.

Here are some examples of what they produced. The first (Figure 7) shows a book made by a parent at a book-making workshop at Jubilee School. This parent invited her child to illustrate the story and they produced the same story in English. So there were two books telling the same story in two languages.

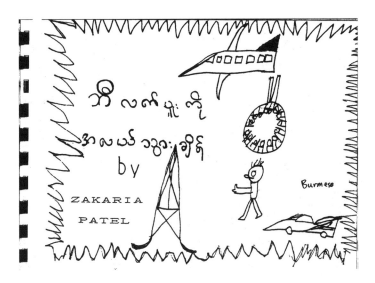

Figure 7

The second (Figure 8) was made by an English-speaking parent who illustrated it herself and it was clearly based on the Meg and Mog stories.

Meg and Mog waved goodbye to Sophie and Phoebe.

They flew off into the evening sky.

Now it was bedtime for Sophie and Phoebe.

Figure 8

Props

Props are essential to enable children to start to be able to talk and think about what they have said and done. This applies to all children and not only to those beginning to learn English. Thinking about the *work that is displayed* on the walls is important and it is worth considering how what you plan to display can help children recall and reflect on what they have done. You may want to make a book of photographs to remember a visit to a fire station or the local shops or a museum or the library. It might be a chart the children have made recording the number of different vehicles they observed passing the setting over a period of time. It could be the recipe of the chapattis they made in class together with the cooking utensils used.

Organisation of the room and the activities in it

Ensure that in your room there are quiet corners so that children can go in there on their own or with a friend or two in order to look at books or to sing or to talk. Children need opportunities to try out language without being assessed or listened to.

Try to ensure that the activities on offer are as meaningful as possible, allowing children to draw on their own experience (including their experience of language) and to see the purpose of what they are doing. For older children there will, of course, be many abstract activities but it is important to try to make these as meaningful as possible to enable children new to English to build on what they have already learned and what they already know.

Learn from the work of Kenner and invite bilingual children to play the role of teacher, perhaps during part of the Literacy Hour. Their teaching would be on some aspect of their first language which they 'teach' to the other children. This enables them to reflect on their own awareness of their first language and to use their second language to discuss this. It enables the other children to see the things that are similar and that are different between languages. This strategy is powerful in developing metalinguistic awareness. Teachers and other adults will benefit too!

SUMMARY

This is the second of two chapters examining how to provide effective classrooms or settings for bilingual children and the focus here has been on effective ways of teaching children English as an additional language. Like the previous chapter this is essentially a practical chapter.

GLOSSARY

Apprenticeship	This is where a child learns alongside an experienced other person – an adult or another child.
Authentic uses of language	This refers to language being used for real purposes in lifelike situations.
Comprehensible input	This refers to ensuring that children are able to understand what is being said to or required of them.

Guided participation	This is a phrase used by Barbara Rogoff to describe the learning she observed in some developing countries where children learn from being alongside experienced others. It is synonymous with apprenticeship.
Meaningful context	Situations or activities where the meaning of the task is embedded in it – such as cooking or planting seeds or buying something in the shops or building a tower.
Silent period	The almost inevitable period where a child new to a language and culture spends time looking and listening and thinking before being willing or able to speak.

Chapter 7

Assessing bilingual learners

In this chapter we raise the issue of confusing those children who have yet to learn English in order to succeed in school and live in society with those children who speak English but seem to have difficulties succeeding in the school or setting.

We consider the importance of assessing bilingual children's language proficiency and examine ways of doing this.

And finally we look at assessing bilingual children who do have learning or behavioural difficulties.

There is a grave tendency to think of children who have English as an additional language also having special educational needs (SEN). Indeed there is evidence to show that bilingual children are over-represented in SEN groups and classes and all this despite a ruling from the Department for Education and Employment (1996: Section 312) which states that

> A child is not to be taken as having a learning difficulty solely because the language (or form of a language) in which he is, or will be, taught is different from a language (or form of a language) which has at any time been spoken in his home.

The aim of this ruling was to ensure that children would not be stigmatised as having special needs when they were simply in the early stages of learning English. So whilst these children have yet to learn a great deal about English in order to succeed in school, they have already learned a great deal *in* their home language(s) and *about* language per se. There are, of course, some bilingual children who do have special educational needs but you should be careful when thinking about the children in your group, to see the difference between the particular needs of those new to English and of those with learning or other difficulties.

Children learning English as an additional language do have special needs only in the sense of needing to learn to use English for both social and academic purposes. Young children learn to use English for social interactions with relative ease. Learning to use English for academic purposes is quite different, more complex and hence takes longer. The issue for educators is knowing what competence the child has in his or her first language(s) and to monitor their developing competence in English.

LANGUAGE PROFICIENCY

You will know that language is crucial to our experience as human beings. It is one of the things that define us as being human and you will recognise the vital role it plays in thought and in establishing and maintaining social contact. We are dependent on one another and effective communication is essential for our successful existence in groups. Frederickson and Cline (2002) identify five language competencies which the competent language user knows and uses. These involve knowing the following:

1 the forms of language that are shared – the sounds of the words and how they go together (i.e. the *phonology* and the *syntax*);
2 the forms that can be used to convey meaning and the ability to understand the meanings of others (*semantics*);
3 the social conventions that determine how people use language to communicate their needs and intentions and understand the needs and intentions of others (*pragmatic competence*);
4 the required styles of communication and the language in order to suit the needs of different audiences and domains (*conversational competence*); and
5 how language changes according to different social and cultural contexts (*sociolinguistic competence*).

Once you disentangle the unfamiliar terms you will realise that this shows us that when we talk about anyone being competent as a language user we are talking about more than the familiar skills of speaking, listening, reading and writing. What we are talking about is a much more social view of language competence which situates each speaker in a complex chain of communication. The chain works like this: the child listens to a partner, understands the intentions and meaning of the partner and responds, and the partner then has to understand the meanings and intentions of the child and so on. Communication is made up of a series of these links in the chain of a conversation or a dialogue or an exchange. It is known that children with SEN may have some difficulties in mastering some or all of these competences. In coming to assess any child's competence it is important to be able to specify what that child can do in terms of this communication chain.

Frederickson and Cline (2002) cite some interesting examples which you may read in their long and fascinating book. Here is one example to think about.

> Four-year-old Susan has been blind from birth. She is more likely, when learning new words, to restrict these to her own experience rather than extend them to new situations. So she will be able to learn the word 'soap' when in the bathroom but it will take her longer than a sighted child to generalise the word to the kitchen or the supermarket.

Bilingual children need to have their language proficiency in all of their languages assessed in terms of the competences outlined above. So this involves going beyond the child's capacity to speak and listen and even beyond the child's abilities to read and write. Language competence must also reflect attitudes and feelings, confidence and the complex analysis of contexts and domains. In thinking about how one might assess a bilingual child's competence you may find the example below helpful.

> Natalya is a Polish speaker now learning English as an additional language. In assessing her competence you would need to know something about her *expertise* which refers to the degree of proficiency in Polish. This means you want to know about her ability to use

Polish words in grammatical sentences in order to communicate her ideas and her needs to someone else and to understand other Polish speakers communicating their needs or intentions. You would also want to know about *affiliation* which refers to affective relationships with the language. This means trying to understand what feelings she associates with her two languages. Does she find Polish better for talking about her feelings and English better for talking about her day to day experiences in the playground? Does she find English better to use when she is doing homework and Polish better when playing with her sister? And finally you would want to know about *inheritance* which refers to the language associated with things like family or community. For Natalya Polish is the language she uses with her family and with her grandparents and community members on return to Poland, but English is the language of her new community.

Bilingual adult students, writing autobiographical accounts about their own language experiences, often note that their children, born in the UK and growing up with two languages, start to reject the language of home in favour of the language of the new community of school and peers. They develop very complex feelings about their languages, often feeling embarrassed to be heard using Urdu or Greek, for example. For them, identification with the peer group seems to be the overriding consideration for some time. It is only when they have their own children that they rediscover the urge to use the language of their families.

We said earlier in this book that being bilingual is more than being the sum of two monolinguals. Bilinguals need not only to be fluent in their languages but also to establish a complex and intricate web of which language is spoken to whom, where and for what purposes. Grosjean (1982) uses the analogy of a high-hurdler and explains it like this. A sprinter can run faster on the flat and a high-jumper can jump higher, but neither can run very fast over obstacles. Monolinguals are the sprinters or the high-jumpers, but the bilingual is the high-hurdler with a unique combination of skills.

THE RUNNER

The monolingual child is like a runner who has acquired the fine skill of running fast on the flat.

THE JUMPER

The bilingual child is not like a child who has two separate skills – running and jumping. Rather this child has to have combined several skills, including language fluency and communicative sensitivity.

You will know that you are required to monitor the language proficiency of all children in your class or setting because it is recognised that children who have language difficulties will struggle with formal learning and thus early identification is seen as important. Often children with severe language difficulties are diagnosed before coming to school or setting. You will encounter many children whose language is a little delayed and you will recognise this where a child speaks like a much younger child or uses a limited vocabulary or struggles to understand what is being said. Such delays are within the range of normal and although you would certainly take note you would not, necessarily, seek intervention. In terms of being alert to more profound language difficulties you might look out for all or any of the following things in the behaviour and speech of the child:

- Difficulty in *keeping track* of a conversation
- *Odd grammatical structures* in speaking or writing
- Failure to understand *words that make logical connections* like 'because' or 'so'
- Tendency to *avoid tasks involving language* and so on.

For the bilingual children in your group you will want to be able to assess their competence in both or all their languages and this may often be extremely difficult for you to do. The *Code of Practice* (2001), used to identify children who have learning difficulties, says that a full assessment of language at an early stage includes finding out about each of the languages spoken, the use children make of them and their proficiency in them. This forms some baseline for assessments that follow. This is a sensible suggestion but in reality is extremely difficult to do. Teachers and practitioners do not have the time or often the skill to be able to do this and a simpler solution might be to ensure that, on entry to school or setting, some important information is collected.

Here is what is done at one primary school in Bradford.

Entry profile

(to be completed with parent or carer accompanied by an interpreter/translator)
What languages do you speak at home

- (a) at meal times
- (b) to your child/children
- (c) to grandparents?

What languages are spoken to your child by

- (a) mother
- (b) father
- (c) siblings
- (d) grandparents?

Can you think of some ways in which the language you use at home is different from English – direction of script, alphabet, symbols, stress patterns?

How long has your child been living in this country?

Has your child been to a school or a crèche or a nursery or anything like that in another country?

Where?

In what language?

Does your child go to any school organised by your community?

What language does s/he speak or learn there?

Is s/he learning to read and write in that language?

You can see that some important information can be gathered like this but to imply that it will give you a full picture of any child's competence in his or her first languages would be misleading.

ASSESSING THE LANGUAGE PROFICIENCY OF CHILDREN LEARNING ENGLISH AS AN ADDITIONAL LANGUAGE

It is important for you to track the child's developing competence in English during the child's time with you in the class or setting. You will want to know that the child is learning English, and is developing confidence in using it in different contexts and with different people and also for academic purposes. Tracking progress in learning English is complex and one of the most useful ways of describing the process is that developed by Hilary Hester.

In *Patterns of Learning* (1990) Hilary Hester devised the stages of English learning which chart progress from being new to English to being a fluent user of English. It is important to remember that children may move into English in very individual ways, and that the experience of first learning English for an older child will be different from that of a younger child. In line with what we have been saying the scales emphasise the social aspects of learning as well as the linguistic. It is apparent that attitudes in the school or setting to children and their languages and cultures will have an effect on their confidence in using both their first and second languages. The stages are as follows:

Stage 1: New to English

The child:

- *Makes contact with another child* in the class.
- Joins in activities with other children, but may not speak. This is the start of what may be a *prolonged silent period*.
- *Uses non-verbal gestures to indicate meaning* – particularly needs, likes and dislikes.
- *Watches carefully* what other children are doing, and often *imitates* them.
- *Listens carefully* and often 'echoes' words and phrases of other children and adults.
- Takes advantage of opportunities for *listening to the sounds, rhythms and tunes of English through songs, rhymes, stories and conversations*. May join in repeating refrain in a story.

- Is *beginning to label objects* in the classroom, and personal things.
- Is *beginning to put words together into holistic phrases* (e.g. 'no come here', 'where find it?', 'no eating that').
- May be involved in classroom learning activities in the first language *with children who speak the same first language.*
- May *choose to use first language only* in most contexts.
- May *be willing to write in the first language* (if s/he can), and if invited to.
- May *be reticent with unknown adults.*
- May *be very aware of negative attitudes* by peer group to the first language.
- May *choose to move into English through story and reading*, rather than speaking.

Case Study: December 2004

Rehana is 6 years old and has been in England for two months. Her first language is Gujarati. She started school a month ago and was very withdrawn at first but then found another Gujarati speaker in the parallel class and made friends with her. This has made playtime bearable for her. In her own class there are no other Gujarati speakers. To date she has been silent in the classroom, not even speaking Gujarati. She watches intently what the other children are doing and sometimes copies them. She listens to stories although it is not clear what she understands. She is very wary of new adults and seems passive although the bilingual teaching assistant (who, sadly, does not speak Gujarati) says that her responses are perfectly acceptable for a child who has recently started school in a new country and a new language.

Stage 2: Becoming familiar with English

The child:

- Shows *growing confidence in using the English* s/he is acquiring.
- Shows *growing ability to move between the languages*, and to hold conversations in English with peer groups.

97

▶ *Uses simple holistic phrases* which may be *combined or expanded to communicate new ideas.*

▶ Is *beginning to sort out small details* (e.g. 'he' and 'she' distinction) but more interested in communicating meaning than in 'correctness'.

▶ Has *increasing control of the English tense system in particular contexts*, such as story-telling, reporting events and activities that s/he has been involved in, and from book language.

▶ *Understands more English than s/he can use.*

▶ Has a *growing vocabulary* for naming objects and events, and is beginning to describe in more detail (e.g. colour, size, quantity) and use simple adverbs.

▶ *Is increasingly confident in taking part in activities with other children through English.*

▶ Is *beginning to write simple stories*, often modelled on those s/he has heard read aloud.

▶ Is *beginning to write simple accounts of activities* s/he has been involved in, but may need, at times, support from adults and other children in her/his first language.

▶ *Continues to rely on support of her/his friends.*

Case Study: July 2005

Rehana has made excellent progress in this, her first year at school in the UK. She is now able to communicate with her peers and with adults, sometimes only in English and sometimes using both languages in one utterance. She has a wide English vocabulary which includes nouns, verbs and adjectives and has moved on from two-word utterances to sentences, often using the correct grammatical constructions but still confusing things like his and her. She has made friends within the classroom and joins in all class activities. She has started to write in English and is able to retell English stories using simple sentences.

Stage 3: Becoming confident as a user of English

The child:

- Shows *great confidence in using English in most social situations*. This confidence may mask the need for support in taking on other registers, often those associated with specialised academic language (e.g. in science investigation, in historical research).
- Shows a *growing command of the grammatical system of English* – including complex verbal meanings (relationships of time, expressing tentativeness and subtle intention with words such as might, could, etc. . . .) and more complex sentence structure.
- Is *developing an understanding of metaphor and pun.*
- *Uses pronunciation which may be very native-speaker-like*, especially that of young children.
- Has a *widening vocabulary from reading* stories, poems and information books and from being involved in maths, and science investigations, and other curriculum areas.
- May *choose to explore complex ideas* (e.g. in drama/role play) in the first language with children who share the same first language.

Case Study: January 2006

Rehana's progress in English has been startling since she started in Year 3. Her pronunciation is very like that of the other children in her class – East London! She has become a compulsive reader and her reading has introduced her to complex sentence structures and the use of things like metaphor and pun. Her writing is very mature and she has taken to writing simple poems and stories. She is able to use words in English that many of the native English speakers do not use yet – words like 'could' and 'might' and 'ought to'. In the playground she is often to be found talking volubly and excitedly in Gujarati with Gujarati speakers from other classes.

Stage 4: A very fluent user of English in most social and learning contexts

The child:

- Has become *a very experienced user of English*, and exceptionally fluent in many contexts. May continue to need support in understanding subtle nuances of metaphor, and in Anglo-centric cultural content in poems and literature.
- Is *confident in exchanges and collaboration with English-speaking peers*.
- Is *writing confidently in English with a growing competence over different genres*.
- *Demonstrates continuing and new development in English drawn from own reading and books read aloud*.
- Often reveals *new developments in own writing*.
- *Will move with ease between English and the first language depending on the contexts* s/he finds her/himself in, what s/he judges appropriate, and the encouragement of the school or setting.

(© Hilary Hester, CLPE)

ASSESSING BILINGUAL CHILDREN WHO HAVE SEN

Children presenting with perceived difficulties in the classroom need to be assessed in some way in order for a diagnosis to be made of what the causes of their difficulties are. In the past children were tested and the tests were often biased in the sense that they used pictures of objects not familiar to the children (for example, a quill pen, an inkwell, a wigwam) or used language that was impenetrable for the children. Now it is less common for such crude tests to be used. Bilingual children, giving cause for concern and possibly needing specialist help, must be identified by the school or setting which should then observe the Code of Practice. This means having to go through a clearly defined process, involving five stages leading up to a formal assessment and statement of those identified as having SEN. You will know that this statement must be published and made available to parents and managers or school governors. You will have, in your school or setting, a designated person sometimes called the Special Educational Needs Coordinator, or SENCO, who must keep a register of all children with special needs and a record of what has been done to meet these needs.

Here is an outline of the five steps set out in the Code of Practice.

Stage 1

This is the initial stage of gathering information and making some assessment of what the particular difficulty is. This is often initiated as the result of a parent, carer or worker expressing some concern about the child's development and is likely to be the stage most of you would be concerned with. It is important at this stage to liaise very closely with parents and to record in detail what the concern is, what steps have been taken and what the results are. It is recommended that practitioners, often together with parents, set targets for the child's progress and that these targets are also recorded. Other professionals may be involved at this stage – people like health visitors, speech therapists and so on. It is also recommended that reviews should be carried out, usually within a six-month period, and that if, after two such reviews, progress is not regarded as satisfactory (i.e. targets have not been met) Stage 2 is reached.

Stage 2

This is the point at which practitioners feel that they need additional specialist advice from people like doctors, specialist teachers for children with hearing or visual impairments and so on. In this stage practitioners are asked to draw up an Individual Education Plan (IEP) for the child and this should include:

- the nature of the child's difficulties;
- any special provision given and by whom;
- any particular programmes followed;
- what help the parents give;
- targets to be achieved by particular dates;
- any medical arrangements or pastoral care;
- the arrangements for monitoring and assessment;
- the arrangements for review of progress.

101

Again, parents need to be kept fully informed and involved and their views should always be taken into account.

Stage 3

During this stage the school or setting can call on additional professional help from people such as educational psychologists, and the responsibility for the child is now shared with any outside agencies called in. A new IEP is drawn up and, again, partnership with parents is essential. If, on review, progress is not satisfactory the child may be referred to the local education authority for a statutory assessment. The setting or school must provide written evidence of all that has been done during Stages 1 to 3.

Stage 4

The local education authority is required to carry out a statutory assessment of the child within 26 weeks of a request to do so by a parent, a worker, a school or an outside agency. This is the point where the school or setting feels unable to promote the child's development within the school or setting.

Stage 5

This is where a formal statement of the child's special educational needs is drawn up by the local education authority once it has established that the child's difficulties:

- are significant and/or complex;
- have not yet been met by the actions taken locally;
- may call for resources which are not available within mainstream education.

This should all be familiar to you but in terms of the potential statementing of bilingual children there are some areas of concern. It is important to remember that the difficulties bilingual children have in the early stages of acquiring English may well be temporary and care should be taken that these children are not inappropriately involved in a process which may be deeply concerning for them and for their parents and carers. Those involved with the child need to allow time (and to remember that bilingual children often pass through a silent period), need to observe the child closely in a range of contexts and need to bear in mind the sequence of learning a second or subsequent language laid out by Hilary Hester and cited above. The best way of observing the progress of bilingual learners is done in what Figueroa (2002) calls an *'enriched, effective classroom'*. This is an environment, often common in nursery classes, where there is a range of activities, where the purpose of an activity is clear and where children can draw on the prior learning and experience. It is in such an environment that it is possible to attribute the child's difficulties to things other than inappropriate teaching.

Baker (2006) reminds us that it is vital to know as much as possible about the child's experiences prior to coming to school or setting and to find out what aspects of learning and achievement are valued by the child's family and culture. Liz Brooker, in her book *Starting School* (2002), carried out a study of the experiences of two groups of children from working-class families during their first year of formal schooling in East London. One group of children came from English-speaking families and the other from Sylheti-speaking Bangladeshi families. Brooker looked at the experiences of the children and at the parallel experiences and thoughts of their parents as their children learned in a reception class which labelled itself as 'child-centred'. One of the most striking findings was that the Bangladeshi parents experienced some cognitive dissonance when being asked to accept some of the values of this so-called child-centred approach. The English-speaking parents paid lip service to recognising that play was the way in which young children learn best, although they had trouble in explaining why this might be so. Bangladeshi parents, on the other hand, felt their children should be properly instructed and believed that they, at home, had the job of instructing their children in religious knowledge, teaching the alphabets and the counting systems of English, Bengali and Arabic. They could not believe that children would learn through play and when the class went on outings many kept their children at home. Outings were seen as the preserve of families and had little to do with learning. There has been a body of research into the views of parents from ethnic minorities on teaching style and what emerges is a clear reluctance to accept that learning can take place through anything other than instruction. Those working with bilingual children need to engage in dialogue with the parents in order to seek their views, to understand them and to persuade them

103

that what their children are doing when they play or paint or act or read or make marks is learning. For many families play and hands-on learning, so prized by this culture, are not recognised as part of learning. Nor, indeed, is encouraging children's curiosity and inviting them to pose questions recognised by some cultures. Often what is valued is what is familiar in the educational experiences of the parents which sometimes means that adults are perceived as authority figures, holding the wisdom and passing it on to the children. Play is something done for pleasure and the links between play and learning are not understood or accepted. The importance of this is that some children may not only encounter feeling strange or different in terms of their language but also in terms of the attitudes of their parents and communities to learning. Educators need to be sensitive to this.

Bilingual children are continually tested in schools in the UK alongside their monolingual peers. You may want to think carefully about how to interpret the scores and whether it is fair to expect bilingual learners to match the language competence of monolingual English speakers on English language tests. We have already seen how the language competences of bilinguals are different from those of monolinguals. Bilinguals, you will remember, demonstrate awareness of more than one language system, show communicative sensitivity in terms of language and domain and have developed metalinguistic awareness. English language tests, in general, do not allow for the particular competences of bilinguals to be reflected in the results. It would seem likely that bilingual learners are disadvantaged in this way.

PLANNING FOR LEARNING IN A BILINGUAL CLASSROOM

Birgit Voss, herself bilingual, ran an extremely well-organised and carefully thought-out classroom for nursery children in an inner London school. She worked very carefully with her support staff and each term planned ahead in great detail. She was very clear that in the staff team there were different viewpoints and strengths and values – not to mention different educational backgrounds and different salaries. Working as a team was clearly vital and thus communication between team members was a priority. Here is what she said about planning for the term ahead.

For the first two weeks of term we have only the eighteen children who were part-time last term. Twelve stay for lunch, six go home and return afterwards. We have facilities to ensure a high-quality lunchtime for twelve children only. Six children sit with a member of staff at each of two tables and lunch is, of course, not simply about food intake. All areas of the curriculum can be covered in that one hour. It is often the time for 'intimate' conversations and children have shared many family secrets and things that troubled them during lunch . . .

From my home visits (made prior to the children starting) I know that some of the bilingual children joining us are very much at the beginning stages of learning English. I make a note of the different languages our little community will be using for the next four months: Gujarati, Bengali, Turkish, Urdu, Cantonese, Persian, Arabic, German and, of course, English. I check these against our present resources. We have cassette and video story-tapes in all the languages but Cantonese. We have plenty of writing samples, newspapers and magazines in Chinese as we had some Chinese-speaking children earlier. When we celebrated Chinese New Year – the Year of the Dog – we stocked up during a visit to the local Chinese supermarket. We also have appropriate clothes, fabrics and home base equipment – and lots of pictures. The parents seemed very open, friendly and cooperative during the home visit. I am sure they would love to make some story-tapes, maybe some songs for us – something to organise.

For the other bilingual children we probably at this stage do not need to prepare anything different from what we normally offer. The way children learn in our class by firsthand experience, building on and extending what they already know, is ideally suited to acquiring another language. Children are encouraged to collaborate with each other and research has shown that bilingual children working and learning with their English-speaking peers get to know English very fast. We provide many opportunities for rehearsal and repetition of natural language patterns, and, of course, we have many stories with additional visual support (things like story props are either two- or three-dimensional). The team is aware that often children in the beginning stages of learning English go through the 'silent' period; and feel confident before they dare to utter the first English word. Bombarding them with direct questions, insisting on a response, can be very intimidating during this time. How often do we teach by asking questions? Even I, who through my own experiences am very aware of this silent period phenomenon (I didn't dare speak an English word for nearly a whole year when I first came to this country!), catch myself asking silly questions, but having done so also provide the answer and do not expect it from the child. There are many opportunities in a busy nursery classroom in which spoken English is not a requirement for participation in an activity.

(Voss in Smidt, 1998: 47–8)

Voss went on to detail some of the activities that would allow bilingual children to fully participate alongside their English-speaking peers. She cited the following:

- *The magnet board which is used for story props or for using photo cut-outs and names. The photo cut-outs are full-length photos of each child cut out and laminated with magnetic tape fixed to the back. Children can use these in any way in which pleases them or meets their needs.*
- *The use of photography to record class events and make books from these. The books sometimes illustrate classroom routines.*
- *Book-making is an ongoing activity and these books are usually aimed at beginner readers and use repetitive language patterns and clear fonts. Sometimes these are translated by parents to make dual language texts.*
- *Some words – mainly greetings – are written up in the book corner and children are sent home with a greeting in their home language.*

Dodwell (1999) tells us that planning for bilingual learning is vital and suggests to practitioners that the language associated with each planned activity needs to be carefully considered. Her approach is far more formal than that of Voss. She suggests that practitioners need to identify target words which the child should learn through the activity and they should introduce these key words in the first language of each child. This is ideal but hardly practical for most of us. But she tells us that there are many dictionaries which have phonetic transcriptions to help English-speaking teachers. Like Voss, Dodwell appreciates the value of first-hand experience and play in helping bilingual children acquire English as an additional language. She identifies the importance of resourcing in the play areas – such things as appropriate dressing-up clothes, cooking implements and tableware, calendars and images and leaflets and newspapers – all reflecting the cultures of the children in the group.

SUMMARY

The issue of assessment and bilingual learners is a complex one largely because the curriculum is so largely language-based. It is important for those working with bilinguals to keep reminding themselves of the cognitive advantages bilingualism itself gives and to try and recognise the considerable achievements bilingual children make as they acquire another language. When testing children – as when teaching them – the more meaningful the context and the input, the more comprehensible the purpose, the more interactive the teaching, the better chance there is that these children will reveal just what they know and can do. This is not to say that there are not bilingual pupils who may have learning difficulties or behaviour problems.

GLOSSARY

Affiliation	This means a link to something. In this context it means the link a learner has to his or her culture or language or religion or values, for example.
Assessment	This is the process of gathering together evidence to show how a learner is progressing and what that learner knows and can do at a particular point in time.
Cognitive dissonance	Where a new idea is encountered that the learner finds troubling because it does not fit in with the learner's previous ideas and learning.
Communication chain	The way communication works, through those involved taking turns to make and share meaning.
Competence	Another word for ability.
Competencies	A specialist term used to talk about the specific abilities involved in using language, for example, effectively.

Conversational competence	The ability to take part in a conversation or a social exchange.
Domain	This refers to where exchanges (including language) take place so school and home are domains, the playground and the classrooms are domains, and so on.
Enriched, effective classrooms	Classrooms which are set out with a range of meaningful activities where the purpose of tasks is clear and which will allow children both to encounter a challenge and also to build on their prior experience and learning.
Expertise	Another word for ability – here relating to the use of vocabulary and grammar in order to understand and be understood.
Generalise	Applying something from one situation to another; in this case knowing that soap is something that occurs in different domains or contexts.
Inheritance	In this context the term is used to define the language used in connection with family and family links.
Metaphor	The way in which one thing is thought to be like another and very important in learning: one of the higher-order cognitive skills, it involves comparing and contrasting.
Phonology	The sound system of a language.
Pragmatic competence	Understanding the rules that govern the practical day-to-day exchanges between people.
Semantics	A synonym for 'meaning'.
Sociolinguistic competence	Understanding how language changes according to things like purpose, syntax, audience, domain and so on.

Chapter 8

Working with the parents of bilingual children: the importance of partnerships

In this chapter we talk, briefly, of why it is important to work closely with parents.

We then turn our attention to working with the parents of bilingual children and consider ways in which we can communicate effectively with them.

We think, too, about how to take on board their views and opinions and to enable them to understand our views and opinions about teaching and learning.

PARTNERSHIPS WITH PARENTS

You will know that establishing close relationships with parents and carers is given much prominence in schools and settings today. It is promoted by the Children Act (1989) and numerous other Acts and documents. This means that, after a long and chequered history of parental involvement with schools, parents are no longer kept at arm's length from the school or setting, but invited in and consulted with. It is a cliché to say that parents know more about their own child than anyone else, but like most clichés it is true. Practitioners and teachers do, of course, get to know children well, but it is important to recognise that their knowledge of any child is limited. The person who sees the child in almost every situation at almost every time of the day and year is the parent. Parents are, indeed, experts when it comes to their own child. With the well-being and the progress of the child at heart, it is essential that those working with the child establish respectful relationships with these experts. Indeed, forming effective parental partnerships is seen as so important in the UK that you can find it included in government guidance. Here is what it says on the Standards site (DFES):

Success in the education of children depends, at least in some part, on the involvement of their parents. If a child sees that their parents are enthusiastic about education, they are far more likely to view their schooling in a positive light, and be more receptive to learning.

To this end, parents should be seen as vital partners in a child's education, as not only can they help in making sure homework is in on time and in giving a child vital coaching and advice out of school hours, but they also determine the child's home environment, where children spend much of their waking hours. Engaging and working with parents is one of the most vital parts of providing children with an excellent education.

Below, you will find a range of suggestions about how you can improve your school's relationship with parents, based on the government's guidance on home–school agreements, and on good practice in schools.

The home–school agreements guidance suggests that governing bodies are encouraged to review their home–school policy. Here are a few points to consider.

- Have you asked parents what they expect from the school?
- What do you expect from parents?
- Have you asked parents what they think of the school?
- How do you involve parents?
- Why do some parents not get involved?
- What can you do to establish an effective working relationship with the 'missing' parents?
- What can you do to help parents to help their child?
- What priority do teachers give to working with parents?
- What does your school do to listen to the views of pupils?

Listed below are some more practical suggestions for things that might help to underpin the developing working relationships encouraged by the agreement.

- Is the main entrance well-signposted so that visitors and parents don't experience difficulty in finding their way to the reception office?
- Is the school foyer welcoming and informative?
- Are the school's signs written in positive language? For example, 'All visitors must report to the school office' can be changed to 'Welcome to . . . . School. Please report to the office.'
- Is there a procedure for ensuring that all written and telephone enquiries from parents are dealt with promptly?
- Are a variety of forms of communication with parents, for example, telephone contact and home visits, encouraged?
- Are parents contacted for positive as well as negative reasons?
- Is there a need to review the quality and appearance of written home–school communication?
- Should consideration be given to the use of 'mail merge' to personalise some letters to parents?
- Do signatures on letters to parents include forenames?
- How much information is given to parents on what pupils are taught?
- Are parents encouraged to help or support their children's learning at school and at home? How much information or training is provided to enable this support to be effective?
- Does the school encourage the use of parents as volunteer helpers?
- Does the school promote any family learning or family fun activities?
- Is parental involvement and support sought for study support programmes?
- Are adult education providers encouraged to organise daytime or out-of-school learning programmes for parents?
- Is value placed on all parents, irrespective of background or ability?
- Does the school have a Home–School Association?
- Is inter-agency collaboration with services that share an interest in children and their families encouraged? Examples of those with whom collaboration is possible include education welfare workers, health workers, adult education

workers, librarians, the police, social services, youth workers, the Travellers' Service, English-as-another-language workers, and voluntary sector workers.

▶ Are collaborative working initiatives with some of these services encouraged by, for example, addressing 'parent education' with the assistance of health and/or youth workers?

The DfES has a website for parents which may be helpful when thinking about ways to work with parents, and especially in providing information which can be given to them easily. It has an entry-point for teachers which suggests ways in which this can be done.

Now you may have found all that rather prosaic and couched in the sort of language which doesn't quite see parents as full partners in this exchange. Contrast it with the approach to parental involvement in some of the nurseries in Reggio Emilia. Carlina Rinaldi (2006) writing about the nurseries for the youngest children (called *nidi*, 'nests') explains that it was only in the late twentieth century that a public institution (in her case the *nido*, in ours schools and settings) started to seek the active, direct and explicit participation in what she calls the 'formulation of the project'. The project is the well-being of the child. In using these very words she indicates how much more advanced the Italian approach to child care and education is than ours. We still assume that parents delegate responsibility to us, the educators, and that parents rarely talk about choice of teaching material (or curriculum) or teaching style with teachers or practitioners for fear that they will be ignored or their children in some way penalised. Rinaldi talks about the centrality not only of a partnership between the child and the educator, but between the child, the educator and the parents – a three-way or triangular set of relationships. For her, the *nido* is the place of relationships and communication and the place where a way of teaching (or pedagogy) is constructed. In other words she is saying that when this three-way set of relationships is working, those involved do not merely carry out instructions and respond to events but actually create an ethos, a teaching style, ways of learning and relating, and do this collaboratively. Going beyond that, the *nido* is integrated into a wider social system and what happens to one aspect affects another. The *nido* needs to be concerned with the well-being of the staff and of the parents as well as of the children. The success of this will depend on the knowledge, the communication and the awareness of all three.

This is quite complex. We all know how families and family relationships and networks have changed over time. We know that what were traditional and settled networks and relationships have become more fragmented. We have many more one-parent households than we had decades ago. We have more immigrant and refugee and asylum-seeking families than we ever had. We have more parents who are older and better educated than they were years ago. Although ours is a wealthy society there is still deep, ingrained poverty in our cities and countryside. Changes in society are evident, too in the areas of Italy about which Rinaldi wrote. She explains how the *nidi* are developing a range of ways to enable parents to learn to trust educators, to enable educators to learn to respect parents and to enable all involved to work on ways to improve communication in this intricate network.

Many parents are still made to feel that they know nothing and that their understanding of their own child may be flawed or limited. This applies particularly to parents whose first language is not English, who have different ways of nurturing and raising their children or experiences very different from those of the policy-makers in the UK (or in Italy). Almost inevitably – and certainly in inner city areas – parents feel threatened by the education system and by authority. These parents find it difficult to have their voices heard and tend to adopt the stance that 'Teacher and playgroup practitioners know best!'

It is essential to always remember that all parents, whatever their culture, language, background, social class or gender, care about their children. Parents who send young children to a nursery or crèche or playgroup do so for many reasons: some because they feel their children will benefit from contact with other children; some because they want their children to have a head start in the education stakes; some because they need or want to work or study. All parents want the best for their children and all parents deserve to be kept informed about how their children are making progress.

COMMUNICATION – PRACTITIONERS TO PARENTS/ CARERS/FAMILIES OF BILINGUAL PUPILS

Educators are used to being the people in control – the ones 'telling' the parents how the child is getting on. Doing this is much easier than managing a situation which is more dialogic – where views are exchanged rather than information imparted. Yet if we are to have proper and equal partnerships with parents this is something we must learn to do. Facing a host of parents at a formal meeting can be daunting for the most confident teacher, particularly when faced with well-informed, confident and articulate middle-class parents or with parents who have trouble understanding what is being said. Such situations are just as daunting for many parents so finding alternatives is something worth considering. There are many ways of involving parents in a dialogue and below you can find some examples of ways that have been tried and found to be effective:

An introductory visit

At Mahatma Gandhi Primary School they have a policy of taking parents on a tour of the classroom or area where the child will be based on admission. This tour is always conducted in the presence of a speaker of the language of the family (sometimes a bilingual teaching assistant, sometimes a parent or an older child who speaks the same language and sometimes someone invited in from the community). You will realise that work has to have gone on before this tour in order to know what the language of the parent/family is and to match this. The tour is always for one parent or carer at a time. The purpose is to explain a little about how the classroom/setting operates, recognising that some things may not be familiar to the parent. It follows from this that the person conducting the tour (often the headteacher) needs to be able to predict what things might be unfamiliar (perhaps the emphasis on play or the presence of sand in the classroom or the sight of children using clay or getting very messy). The headteacher emphasises that the focus of the visit is on the learning of the child – so the explanation of why something is happening needs to be very clear about how it will help the child learn. Here are two incidents she gives to highlight this:

1   A Vietnamese parent looked very worried about the sand tray in the reception class and made a comment to the translator who then explained that in Vietnam sand is often regarded as being dirty and polluted. The head was able to allay fears explaining that the sand in the classroom comes from specialist educational

suppliers and is very clean, but went on to say that children can learn a great deal about important concepts like 'full' and 'empty', 'heavy' and 'light', 'wet' and 'dry', by having time to play in the sand.

2 A father from Iran was concerned that children doing PE in the hall and wearing shorts and T-shirts included both boys and girls. The headteacher said that she recognised that this was not common in some cultures but that in English primary schools boys and girls learn together. She went on to say that PE gives both boys and girls opportunities not only to develop physical skills but also to understand about many mathematical concepts including comparison (faster, slower; higher, lower), sequencing, pattern, space and so on. She emphasised that where boys and girls learn together they develop respect for one another and self-confidence in working in groups.

Offering different times for coming into school/setting

At the Nelson Mandela Primary School the staff decided that they wanted one member of staff to take additional responsibility for home–school liaison. The person appointed felt it was important to find out from parents when would be a good time for them to come up to the school to find out more about the school, and about their own child, and to meet other parents. She found a very wide range of needs and preferences. A group of Bangladeshi women said they could never come out when it was dark. A group of Polish parents preferred evening meetings with a crèche for children. Working parents wanted meetings after school. Parents at home with younger children wanted to be able to come in during the school day and to have something on offer for the younger children. The school is still trying to meet all these needs but to date has offered parents the following:

1 The opportunity to come into classrooms to help out, putting their children in a specially organised crèche

2 Setting aside time on one day a week when parents can come in and talk with educators after school between 3.30 and 6.00 p.m.

3 An early morning time to come in and talk to the home–school liaison teacher about any incidents or concerns that have arisen (8.15–9.00 a.m.)

4 Termly meetings for the parents of children in each class held before school, after school and in the evening.

Social and educational events

The Mary Seacole Day Nursery has put in place a series of educational events ranging from inviting parents in to 'play' themselves whilst someone goes round and talks to them about what they are learning, to showing parents DVDs of children working, learning, playing, talking. Parents were very tentative about these at first but the events have become increasingly popular and the nursery tries to ensure that there are interpreters always on hand.

The Whittington School offers a range of social events. These include the traditional jumble sale and summer fête but also a Diwali Festival of Lights evening, an evening of Turkish music and food, an annual book fair, a rock and roll evening for parents and children, and many others.

Seeking the views of parents

This is arguably the most difficult but also the most important thing to do. Bilingual parents need to be invited to become involved in meetings to do with the curriculum, in becoming school governors and in applying for posts at school requiring their particular skills. Parents can be invited in to consider whether the resources in the school or setting reflect their culture or not. They can be invited to consider the activities on offer and see if they can find in them links to the experiences of their children and appreciate what the children will learn from these. They can be consulted about potential sites for visits and be invited to join in.

The child, the family, the community

It sometimes becomes apparent that a particular family is having difficulties often relating to poverty, lack of opportunity, discrimination, isolation or culture shock. The school or setting is often not in the position to do anything directly to remedy these conditions but it can put families in touch with agencies which may be able to help. Some schools have started offering adult classes in the school during the school day where parents can learn English or learn a skill which might help them apply for a job.

OTHER VOICES

Despite the good intentions of practitioners, parents who have English as an additional language often find it difficult to express their views on what is happening to their children. Babette Brown, in her book *Unlearning Discrimination in the Early Years* (1998), gives us some vivid examples of this.

> A mother arrives early to collect her baby from the crèche. The baby's carer leaves her to cry while she attends to another child. The mother complains to the carer, explaining that in her country crying babies are always picked up. The carer gives an explanation which includes saying that in this country we 'do not believe in spoiling babies' (p. 111). The mother is not happy with this but feels she can say no more. Her daughter starts to cry when left in the mornings and eventually the carer talks again to the mother, this time to find out what is going wrong at home.

If you think about this you will realise that the carer, believing absolutely in her own training and knowledge, does not hear what the mother says and cannot accept that the fault might lie within the crèche rather than within the home. Brown uses this example as a case study, inviting the reader to consider different responses of the carer to the parent.

A second case study in the same book relates to what happened in a family centre where a group of parents from a particular community placed amulets around the necks of their babies to protect them from illness and other danger. This was customary within their community but against health and safety regulations in the family centre. Brown cites what happened in a staff meeting which discussed how to address the issues. Staff responses included negative comments about 'superstition' and some members of staff urging a firm hand in insisting that centre rules be upheld. The final outcome was very positive with staff agreeing to talk to parents and to listen to their views.

117

Rinaldi reminds us that there is no such thing as 'the parent', rather there are people who are, amongst other things, the parents of a child or children in the school or class or setting. These people have had their own experiences and developed their own values and ideas, often drawn from cultures and communities other than the host community. They have developed complex webs of relationships and interactions and play different roles in and beyond their own communities. Rinaldi states that these parents should be credited with

> having an educational sensibility toward and concern about the child, albeit sometimes unexpressed or which we may be unable to see. We need to learn to see the parents' explicit and implicit needs and respond to them with new and effective answers.
>
> (2006: 36)

This is a powerful and important reminder to us all that we have to be the ones to make the sometimes enormous efforts required to enable these people to let us hear their voices. Here are some of them:

The headteacher insisted that one of us should stay with Felicia for her first few days in the nursery. I explained the difficulties I had because I would be starting my teacher training course during the first week and suggested that perhaps my mother could come in my place. The headteacher was very anxious that we set up a good relationship from the beginning and she agreed that Felicia's grandmother could stay with her. And it worked really well, despite the fact that my mother spoke no English at all at the time. She still told me exactly what Felicia had done and how she was getting on.

We were invited to a meeting at the school about the importance of fathers in their children's lives and education. I didn't want to go. My English is not good and in our community fathers earn the money and go to work. Of course I love my Hamid and want him to do well. In the end I agreed to go and took my friend from work with me because he is really bilingual. It was a very small meeting, only for the parents of new children in one class, and there was a translator there and it was really interesting. In the end I even said something and felt very pleased with myself. As a result I often take Hamid to school and really enjoy going into the room and seeing him with his friends. I like to see into his life.

Food is very important in the *nido*. And I was so pleased when we were invited to come to a special workshop run by the cook and where we – new children and new parents – cooked a meal together. When we had finished cooking we all ate together and it was a wonderful opportunity to meet other parents and to start feeling as though this was our *nido*. That was the beginning of our daughter's career in education and because it was so positive we felt able to talk to her carers and teachers in the *nido* and afterwards in the schools she attended. A good start was so important for us all.

At the nursery school our granddaughter attends they decided to have a 'grandparents' day' and we were invited to come in and play with the children. I was very nervous about doing this. For us play is something children do – not adults – and it felt really odd to be asked to go and play. But when we got there lots of interesting things had been set up and the children took us round and showed us what was what – and in the end I played with Leila and got dressed up in the clothes she found with me. One of the nursery workers took a photograph of me all dressed up. I felt silly! Next day Leila brought home a little book she had made at school and I was in the book, wearing the clothes and looking very happy. We still have the book although Leila is now 11 years old.

I was worried that Sipho was being bullied at school. He became very weepy and didn't want to go in the mornings and finally told us that two boys picked on him and called him names. I went to find my neighbour who also has a child at the school and we went early one morning to see the headteacher. She was really helpful and listened carefully to what we had to say – even calling in the bilingual teaching assistant to help when our English ran out. I don't know what she did. She spoke to the two other boys and to their parents, I think. All I know is that Sipho is now happy to go to school and is making friends. I also know that I can go into that school and talk when I need to.

They have a programme of meetings for parents at my child's primary school. We are all asked to nominate the best time of day for us and a crèche is always provided for the children and translators are always there. The staff select one particular theme to talk about and let us know in advance so we can think about any questions we have. The staff do a small presentation – using examples or a film or video – and then there is time to talk. The groups are always small – no more than 8 parents at a time – and the meetings are short. We have had meetings on many subjects. We learned about why children take books home to share with us and what we can do to read to and with our children. And there was a meeting about what the children learn during PE and during outdoor play. We had one about rhymes and songs when we were asked to sing some songs and teach them to the other parents. After each meeting we can go into the class at any time to watch what is going on or to help where we can. It is a very open system and I think we are all beginning to trust the school.

These parents – some in the UK and some in Reggio Emilia – show what can be achieved where work is done to listen to their views and take seriously their experiences.

SUMMARY

In this chapter we have looked at why it is important to establish genuine dialogic partnerships with parents, including with parents who may, themselves, have little English. We have looked at ways of making these parents feel that the school or setting the child attends is a place for them as well as for their children and we have looked at some case studies illustrating how some successful partnerships are being built.

GLOSSARY

Dialogic	An exchange in which both parties have a voice and want to hear one another.
Nido	An Italian word which means, literally, 'nest' but which is the name given to the child care centres for babies. The plural of the word is *nidi*.
Pedagogy	The art or science of teaching.

Chapter 9

Language and thought

In this chapter we examine the importance of language itself in terms of thinking and learning.

We then look at the role of the home and the community in terms of children's cognition.

We end with looking at the role of the school or setting in terms of children's cognition.

LANGUAGE: MORE ABOUT THINKING AND LEARNING

Can a young child who has not yet acquired her or his first language think? We are all so dependent on language – on using words, written or spoken – to phrase our thoughts, ask our questions, express our ideas and voice our opinions that we may find it difficult to think about whether or not it is possible to think without language. Much of this depends on how we define language. The Cambridge Dictionary defines language as '*a system of communication consisting of sounds, words and grammar, or the system of communication used by the people of a particular country or profession*'. You may find this a very limited definition. Think about how symbolic systems other than sounds and words may also be regarded as languages if we widen the definition. There is the language of mathematics and the language of music, for example. Both use symbols combined together according to specific and defined rules (equivalent to their own grammars) and these are used to communicate thoughts and ideas and relationships and feelings. The essence of language seems to be twofold: that it is symbolic and that its primary purpose is communication. Add to that that it is rule-bound and that it is creative (think of how poets use language) and you have a workable definition.

Thought, again, is a word with multiple uses and multiple meanings. The sense in which it is being used here is in terms of intellectual activity or cognition. And the question which starts this chapter is asking whether young children who have not yet acquired their first language can think. There is a photograph, now famous, showing a very young child placing his ear next to a photograph of a watch. This was taken in the days when watches still ticked. What was the child doing? What prompted this pre-verbal child to 'listen' to a photograph? Was this random behaviour or does it illustrate a pre-verbal child expressing, through his actions, his thoughts? Would you think it unlikely that the child might be thinking *'This is a watch like my mum's. Does it tick like my mum's? Let me listen to find out.'*?

One of the most important theorists in the field of language and thought was Vygotsky and in his work he considered some of what he called the 'higher psychological functions' such as attention and memory. He believed that a key feature of these higher functions is that they are mediated by the use of signs. So using signs or symbols helps us to remember and to hold things in our heads. Some years ago it was common to tell someone to tie a knot in their handkerchief in order to remember something. The knot acts as a sign or symbol, allowing the person to remember something. It stands for or represents the thing to be remembered. This is important because it transforms or changes remembering from a process dependent on direct stimulation from the environment to a process that can be voluntarily regulated and reflected on. It is almost as though you have made a picture of the thing to be remembered which you keep in your head.

Vygotsky was interested in the links between speech and thought. He talked about what he called pre-intellectual speech (which was speech before the emergence of thought) and pre-verbal thought (which was thinking before the emergence of talk). Children, under the age of about 2, demonstrate that they do both. They use vocal activity in interaction to communicate their feelings and emotions and to establish and maintain social contact. They are also capable of goal-directed or purposeful activity which does not require speech.

Here are some examples:

▶ Amina, involved in a peekaboo game with her carer, joins in with the 'boo' by laughing aloud to show her pleasure (using vocal activity to join in and show the emotion of pleasure).

▶ Amina drags a chair over to the shelf near the window of her room and climbs onto it to reach her favourite toy duck (goal-directed activity without speech).

Some time later children demonstrate what Vygotsky called 'practical intelligence'. This is where the child uses syntax (grammar) and logical forms of language which have parallels in her or his problem-solving activities but may not be linked to them in any particularly useful way.

Here is an example to illustrate this:

Liam is drawing on a piece of paper, using a thick blue felt pen. As he draws he chants: 'Ooh, a thick blue line. Very nice. Thick and blue. I like blue. It's my best colour. Except for red [changes pen] which is also my best. And gold. I love gold.'

You can see how Liam is using spoken language to parallel what he is doing but not really to reflect on or think about what he is doing or to solve any problems he has set himself. It is as though he needs both to do something and to say something in parallel.

Later still children move on to using external symbolic means – speech or other cultural tools – to help them solve a problem. Vygotsky talked a lot about tools and by tools he meant things like the everyday tools we use such as pens and pencils but also things we might be surprised to find called tools – such as words and paintings and music. And because he was interested in how ideas and knowledge were passed on from generation to generation, he was interested in the particular tools that define a culture. For Vygotsky, then, these artefacts or cultural tools themselves change mental functioning and affect thinking. The examples below illustrate these ideas.

▶ The book the child hears read to her creates pictures in her head which change her thinking. (The book is the cultural tool.)

123

> The marks the child sees an adult make on paper raise questions in the child's head about what it is the adult is doing and change her thinking. (The writing is the cultural tool.)

> The ring tone of the mobile phone makes the child wonder whose voice might be on the other end. (The mobile phone is the cultural tool.)

It is at this stage that we often overhear children talking aloud as they solve problems or describe their actions.

Mohammed arrives in the nursery and announces that he is going to build a tower from the top down. The teacher is very interested in what he does and watches and records what happens.

Goes to fetch small ladder. Gets Avril to help him set it up.

M: Please put it here, Avril. Just on the carpet so the tower will be right in the middle. Now I need to get some blocks to start the tower. I am going to take two of these big flat ones because they will look really nice at the top. They could be like a helipad.

Picks up two flat blocks, holds them in one hand and climbs up the ladder.

M: Nearly ready now!

Reaches the top – stretches out his hand and stops.

M: Oh, no! It isn't going to work, is it? Because when I let go the blocks won't stay where I want them. They are going to fall. Oh no!

(Personal observation, 2006)

You can see how this talking out loud but not to anyone else is different from the sort of talking aloud encountered in the example given about Liam. The child here is not talking parallel to an activity but in order to identify and solve a problem. Some authors call this monologuing and once it becomes internalised Vygotsky called it *inner speech*. The internalisation marks the point when the thinking required for problem-solving has been established. So language becomes something that is used to reflect on action and develop thought rather than as a prerequisite for problem-solving. In other words children become able to use speech and language as tools in their problem-solving because speech allows them to reflect on and consider what they are doing. In time language becomes a more and more useful term for abstract thought.

In essence what we learn from this is that:

- thought can take place before children have acquired their first language;
- in order for children to be able to reflect on what they have done or discovered it is essential that they have acquired speech and language;
- it is this which allows them to learn from what they have done.

So language may not be a precursor of thought but is essential for cognitive development. Vygotsky saw language as one of the most important *'psychological tools'* that human beings have access to. Others included making maps, drawing diagrams, counting, using mnemonics and so on. Having language is essential for learning. And human beings appropriate language and all other psychological tools from their society and from their culture. This is very important because it means that we all have different ways of learning related to how we were reared, nurtured, related to, communicated with and taught. Now we may not have access to understanding the monologues of young bilingual children but we can be certain that they also use this inner speech as a tool to help them in identifying and solving problems.

A great deal of what children are required to learn throughout their schooling depends on language. To understand science or history or geography requires the ability to understand what is being said, to read required texts, to reflect on underlying concepts and to feed back. Much of this is dependent on language. Assessment of children's progress throughout their schooling also depends to a large extent on language. You have only to think about the SATS or GCSE exams to see this. There is evidence that bilingual children may well be wrongly described as not being effective learners purely because they may have little access to using the language which underpins the concepts and experiences internalised during their formative years. Those bilingual learners who are invited to use their stronger language throughout their formal education are likely to fare better.

Vygotsky believed that children not only constructed meaning from all their experiences but that they did so through interactions with other people. For him, learning, including learning a language, was a deeply social phenomenon. Through using cultural tools and in interaction with more experienced others children are inducted into the language and the ways of their communities. One of the most influential concepts in Vygotsky's work was that of the *zone of proximal development*. This was perceived to be the gap between what a learner could do on his or her own and what the same learner might do with the assistance of another and more experienced person – adult or child. Bruner called what the more experienced learner does *scaffolding*. Scaffolding is what adults or more expert learners do when they support a learner taking the next step in learning. This helps the learner to move from *dependence* on this help to *independence*. The analogy to a scaffold (used to create a structure to help workers reach areas they could not safely reach without it) makes this clear. We are primarily interested in scaffolding language and what happens here is that the educator knows just where the child is linguistically and understands how to move the child forward. It is through sensitive scaffolding that new understandings are possible through collaboration with peers or adults. No task is simplified. Rather the teacher or more expert learner – child or adult – offers the scaffold and when the concept has been grasped, the problem solved, the level of comprehension reached, the scaffold is removed.

We have looked very briefly at the links between language and thought and seen how important language is throughout schooling. Any child being educated in England needs to become proficient in English but it seem highly probable that every child being educated in England and having another language or languages in which she or he learned many concepts should have access to that language to assist their learning. We have seen, too, how children learn using the tools of their own cultures (all children have many cultures and belong to different communities) and through their interactions with more experienced others – children or adults.

LEARNING AND USING LANGUAGE AT HOME AND AT SCHOOL

You may be well aware of the fact that educators often hold negative views towards other languages and dialects and there continues to be a prejudice amongst some teachers that children coming from bilingual homes, homes where people speak non-standard English or working-class homes are at a disadvantage. These beliefs have a long history, some of it dating back to the work of people like Basil Bernstein and Joan Tough in the 1970s. Based on their observation of the failure of children from homes like these to thrive in schools they posited a deficit view of language. Bernstein described middle-class families as talking about things in the past, in the present and in the future, whereas he suggested that working-class families talked about things in the here and now. In his eyes this offered a more restricted use of language, since being able to recall and predict were, for him, higher cognitive functions. He coined the terms *restricted code* to describe the language used in working-class homes and *elaborated code* to describe the language of middle-class homes. He did not seek to examine what happened in schools but laid responsibility at the feet of parents and families. It should be added here that he later changed his views and that his work with regard to trying to improve opportunities for all children was significant. In the USA these deficit views of language were challenged by Labov who examined the language used on the streets by black high-school children in New York. His piece 'The logic of non-standard English' (1972) showed that although these children certainly used a language that was different from standard English, it was a language that allowed children to be articulate, fluid and logical. They certainly used this street language to explain their ideas, pose their questions, suggest solutions and describe feelings and sensations.

Labov's ideas influenced the work of two British researchers, Tizard and Hughes (1984), who turned their attention to looking at the language used within families and comparing it with the language used by teachers and others in educational and care settings. Their research showed that all the parents in their study (who came from different socio-economic groups) used language effectively to their children and with their children. They observed that language within the homes centred on real situations and took place as part of daily life. Parents were tuned in to what their children said, needed and already knew.

127

What happened in the verbal exchanges within the home was a genuine interaction with parent and child each sometimes initiating the exchange and sometimes responding. The language used was absolutely suited to learning since it revolved around making sense of the world, communicating with others, sometimes solving problems or asking questions or describing feelings and events. By contrast, when they turned their attention to the language used by teachers and others in reception classes they found something deeply worrying. They found that exchanges were no longer based on a genuine dialogue, related to what the child was interested in or concerned about. Rather teachers tended to question children, often having a particular answer in their minds which they wanted the children to give them. Perhaps this seems familiar to you:

Child:	Can you cut this in half for me?
Teacher:	What do you want me to do?
Child:	Cut it.
Teacher:	You want me to cut it in two pieces? Two . . . (She wants the child to give her the word 'halves'.)
Child:	[silence]
Teacher:	If I cut it into two pieces and each is the same size what have you got?
Child:	[silence]
Teacher:	You've got two . . .?

The teacher was so intent on getting the 'right' answer that she completely ignored the fact that the child had actually used the word 'half' in her initial request. And the effect on the child of this persistent questioning was to reduce her to silence. You can see from this that Tizard and Hughes begin to shift the responsibility for the perceived failure of some groups of children from the language of the home to the language of the school.

Still later Gordon Wells (1986) carried out an extensive longitudinal study on the language of homes of young children in Bristol. A longitudinal study involves looking at the same group of children over a sustained period of time. In this study microphones were attached to the children (with the prior agreement of parents!) and these were switched on randomly by computers so that neither the children nor their parents knew which conversations were being recorded. Wells found that all families used language in order to make and to share meanings and that, although the type of language and the subjects discussed varied from family to family, all children acquired a language which enabled them to think and to learn and to talk and to solve problems. So Wells, like Tizard and Hughes, situated some of the problem away from the homes and families of children.

Some of the studies of the perceived failure of groups of children in our education system come from the work of people like Bourdieu. He was a Marxist sociologist who examined aspects of society in terms of things like power and class. In Marxist theory *capital* is power which is acquired through labour or work. If you work and earn a salary, that salary is your capital and you can use it to acquire more capital in terms of a place to live, possessions and so on. It is capital that forms the foundation of the class system and social structure in many societies. Bourdieu believed that capital should also have a symbolic component – so that it went beyond the economic definition. By symbolic capital he meant things like cultural, social and linguistic facts which can either benefit individuals or hold them back. Like many theorists his writing is difficult to understand because of the dense language he used. We will take time to define some of the terms he used.

- *Cultural capital* can be loosely defined as being 'what people know'. Perhaps you are studying for a qualification and when you have completed your studies part of your cultural capital will be what you have learned.
- *Fields* are things like 'from home to school' or places where things take place, or exchanges are held.
- *Social capital* can loosely be defined as 'who people know'. You will be familiar with name-dropping – the habit of inserting the names of famous people or current celebrities into conversation in order to impress people. The people you know may well contribute to your social capital.
- *Habitus* is a system of dispositions or habits or attitudes which explain the differences we see in all societies between and within groups. Put crudely, children with a disposition to enjoy formal education and learning are more likely to succeed in schooling. Habitus is acquired by individuals and by groups through experience and it is the product of the history of the family or the individual and of their class and cultural context. Within the concept of habitus there is the

concept of *family habitus*. The family habitus of middle-class children in the United Kingdom is likely to be closer to the habitus valued and recognised by teachers.

This is an analysis which does not focus purely on language but sees language as part of culture and part of identity. Bourdieu's use of the concept of cultural capital was a social and cultural analysis of the reasons for the failure of individuals and groups. It situated the reasons within an economic and power framework and specifically stated that failure was not the result of lack of natural aptitude. In other words, certain groups of children may struggle at school because of the effects of poverty or the impact of prejudice, not because of lack of ability. Prout (2005) reminds us that Bourdieu's theories do not fully allow for children being active agents in their acquisition of capital and in their abilities not only to appropriate but also to transform or change culture.

Children inhabit complex cultural worlds and to each new field or context children bring a store of cultural capital. You will realise that where the cultural capital children bring is close to that valued and held by an institution (for example, the classroom), children are likely to be advantaged. Their cultural capital is accessible to their educators. Where children bring cultural capital that is divergent from that of their educators, the educators do not know what to recognise and value.

The habitus of 'now' is the sum total of the culture and class history of the individual and family.

LIVING IN SIMULTANEOUS WORLDS

We have considered the fact that millions of children throughout the world are speakers of more than one language and many of them have to come to understand and use the symbolic systems of these different languages. In some recent writing the word 'syncretic' occurs and is used to mean the creative transformation of culture. Syncretic studies sees development as a creative process wherein people, including children, reinvent culture, drawing on their resources, old and new. Speakers of languages other than English going to school in England clearly have to deal with the host and dominant language (the language of power, of education, of government and of the media) and to find ways of being able to maintain and use their home languages. There is potential here for dissonance as we saw earlier in the story of Antti.

What the syncretic approach tells us is the following:

1 All children are members of different cultural and linguistic groups and actively seek to belong to these groups in a way that is not linear but is dynamic, fluid and changing.
2 Children do not remain in the separate worlds defined by their cultural group, but move between these worlds. According to Kenner (Kenner and Kress, 2003) they live in 'simultaneous' worlds. So a child is a member of the cultural group of her family but is also actively creating the cultural group of her setting or classroom.
3 As children are members of different groups they change or syncretise or transform the languages and narrative styles, the role relationships and learning styles appropriate to each group and then transform the cultures and languages they use to create new forms.
4 Children who are fortunate enough to interact in practices which are multilingual (where more than one language is involved) and multicultural (where more than one culture is involved) are able to call on a wider range of metacognitive processes, particularly with regard to language itself.

All children seem able to live in more than one world and to adapt their language style and their behaviour according to where they are and who they are with. For bilingual children there is the added dimension of adapting their languages to the audience and the context. Stuart Hall (1992) has pointed out that language and culture keep on changing and so the worlds of children cannot be regarded as fixed and un-changing. Children keep having to create or alter identities as they move between the different and changing worlds of home and school or setting, home and the street or playground, the home of grandparents and the home with siblings. This sounds as though those bilingual children's existence is fragmented but some recent research suggests that this is not the case. Jean Mills (2001) interviewed third-generation children of Pakistani origin and found that they could define themselves as having different identities that coexisted easily. It was as though they defined themselves as Pakistani-English, for example.

Kenner asks the question as to whether we should now be think-ing about simultaneous worlds rather than multiple worlds and she is thinking particularly about those children who grow up with one or more languages from birth or an early age and who begin to become literate in more than one language and spend their time in environments which are multicultural and multilingual. She suggests that, for these children, it is difficult to define their first language, and their second or subsequent languages. It is difficult to define which is their stronger language since they have developed the linguistic competence to use languages for different purposes and with different audiences, so strength of language is dependent on context.

Here are some comments, collected from young adults, to illustrate this:

> I can't really tell you which my strongest language is. I use Bengali with my husband: it is the language of love for me – and that is pretty important. I use Hindi with my cousins and their children. I don't know how this came about – it just sort of happened. English, of course, for schooling and reading academic books but I choose to read in Bengali. I love watching films in Bengali, but also watch *EastEnders* every day.

> We speak Polish at home but my children are speaking more and more English and sometimes I respond in English and sometimes in Polish. The children speak Russian to their grandma, English to one another and read books in all three languages. I read an English newspaper but choose to watch Polish DVDs when I can get them.

> I can read Arabic but don't know what it means. I read Farsi with ease, English with more difficulty. When I write by hand I do it in Farsi but on the computer I use English. I sometimes switch between Farsi and English in one sentence and my children laugh at me – although they also do that. They love to watch Farsi cartoons on DVD but *Blue Peter* in English.

> My first language – I have been told – was Greek. But I grew up in Cyprus and in those days had some friends who spoke Turkish so I learned that too. Then at school we learned English and at university I learned Cantonese. I feel that I have a special interest in languages and enjoy learning about different systems and different grammars. I am planning to learn Icelandic because I have the possibility of

going there to work. I find learning languages easy. The way I do it is to get DVDs and watch them in a different language, listening to it whilst I read the subtitles in English. In this way I learn the sounds and patterns whilst still being able to access the meaning.

Kenner goes on to suggest that whilst many of these children experience simultaneity at home this may not be true – yet – of schools and settings. At home it seems likely that simultaneity will be sponsored by parents who want their children to learn and use English, but also want and need their children to retain their first language. Often these are the families that send their children to community language schools precisely because they want the children to retain their mother tongue. For some fortunate children simultaneity will also apply to their schools or settings. For these children the existence of other languages will be recognised and celebrated in genuine recognition of the benefits for all of doing this.

SUMMARY

In this penultimate chapter we have revisited some material discussed earlier in the book in order to confirm and elaborate it. We have considered Vygotsky's work on language and thought and considered the importance for all learners of having their learning scaffolded. We ended by looking at some research on the type of language used in homes and communities and at school or settings in order to try and explain the failure of some groups in our schooling system. We also examined possible ways in which schools and settings can ensure that all children can be active members of possible simultaneous groups.

GLOSSARY

Cognition	This is another word for thinking.
Cultural capital	A term used by Bourdieu to describe what people know.
Dispositions	Attitudes or ways of thinking.

Elaborated code	The term used by Bernstein to describe the language used in middle-class homes which, he said, referred to the past and to the future as well as to the present.
Fields	A term used by Bourdieu to talk about where things happen or take place; largely synonymous with domains.
Habitus	Also used by Bourdieu, to describe a set of dispositions which explain some of the differences we see in all societies between groups and within groups.
Precursor	Something that comes before something else.
Prerequisite	A requirement that comes before something else .
Psychological tools	A term used by Vygotsky and more or less synonymous with cultural tools: the things developed within cultures in order to assist thinking.
Reflect on	To think about or consider.
Restricted code	The term used by Bernstein to describe the language of working-class homes which, he believed, was restricted to talking about the here and now.
Social capital	Bourdieu's term for talking about who people know in the sense of being able to contribute to social capital.
Zone of proximal development	Vygotsky said that this was the gap between what a child could do unaided and what the child might do with help.

Bilingual education: why should we bother?

This book has been written for those of you working with children and the intention is that it should be for those of you working with *all* children – monolingual, bilingual and multilingual. The world in which we now live is a world where the word and the reality of globalisation are ever-present – in our newspapers, on television, on our streets, in our schools and in our homes. One of the aspects of globalisation that has implications for all of us involved with care and education is the increasing movement of people from one country to another. People move for a range of reasons, as we have already said – some for personal betterment, some to escape dreadful events in their home countries, some filling gaps in the labour market. One of the obvious effects of this mass mobility is that our schools and settings become more and more linguistically, culturally, racially and religiously diverse. In cities like London and Bradford this diversity has a long history but in some of our smaller cities and certainly in rural areas this is something new. Newness often brings with it fear and opens up the possibility for manipulation by groups with a particular agenda or an inability to move beyond seeing new things as anything other than problematic.

What is happening here is that there is a growing move to deal with this perceived 'problem' in a way designed to make it just go away. The idea is to adopt a policy of assimilation into the mainstream of society. The effect of this will be to make everyone 'the same'; to remove cultural and linguistic diversity. This approach is currently dominant in most European and North American countries and although it sounds fine – let's all be the same! – the reality is that it violates the rights of children to have an appropriate education and it threatens to disrupt communication between children and their parents and grandparents and ancestors. More than that, it does not allow for a fundamental tenet of good educational practice – that of building on previous knowledge and experience. Where we force children into learning and using only English we are, as Cummins says, 'contradicting the very essence of education'.

We now live in a multilingual and multicultural country. Our children's children are likely to live in an even more diverse world. It is up to us, as educators, to educate this generation of children so that they are able to relate to people from other places, speaking other languages, holding values different from ours and believing things we do not believe. The way to do this is to remember what we know about why it matters to support the use of first language.

WHAT WE KNOW

1   Bilingualism has positive effects on children's linguistic and educational development.
2   The level of a child's mother tongue is a strong predictor of his or her second-language development.
3   The promotion of mother tongue in the school or setting helps to develop not only mother tongue but also the child's abilities in the majority or host language.
4   Time spent on teaching through the mother tongue does not damage a child's academic development in the majority or host language.
5   Children's mother tongues are fragile and easily lost in the early years of schooling if they are not respected and recognised and used.
6   To reject a child's language in the school or setting is to reject the child himself or herself.

(Drawn from the work of Jim Cummins)

Bibliography

Abbott, L. and Nutbrown, C. (eds) (2001) *Experiencing Reggio Emilia: Implications for Pre-school Provision*. Buckingham and Philadelphia: Open University Press

Aw, T. (2005) *The Harmony Silk Factory*. London: Harper Perennial

Baker, C. (2006) *Foundations of Bilingual Education and Bilingualism*, 4th edn. Clevedon: Multilingual Matters

Bourdieu, P. (1977) *Outline of a Theory in Practice*. Cambridge: Cambridge University Press

Brooker, L. (2002) *Starting School – Young Children Learning Cultures*. Buckingham and Philadelphia: Open University Press

Brown, B. (1998) *Unlearning Discrimination in the Early Years*. Stoke on Trent: Trentham Books

Bruner, J. S. (1982) 'Formats of language acquisition', *American Journal of Semiotics* 1(3): 1–16

Bruner, J. S. (1983) *Child's Talk: Learning to Use Language*. Oxford: Oxford University Press

Bruner, J. S. (1986) *Actual Minds, Possible Worlds*. Cambridge, MA: Harvard University Press

Bruner, J. S. (1996) *The Culture of Education*. Cambridge, MA: Harvard University Press

Centre for Applied Linguistics (2001) *Expanding Educational Opportunity in Linguistically Diverse Societies*. Washington, DC: Centre for Applied Linguistics.

Chomsky, N. (1972) *Language and Mind*. New York: Harcourt Brace Jovanovich

Chomsky, N. (1975) *Reflections on Language*. New York: Random House

Cummins, J. (1980) 'The entry and exit fallacy in bilingual education', *NABE Journal* 4(3): 25–59

Cummins, J. (1996) *Negotiating Identities: Education for Empowerment in a Diverse Society*. Ontario: California Association for Bilingual Education

137

Cummins, J. (2000) *Language, Power and Pedagogy: Bilingual Children in the Crossfire*. Clevedon: Multilingual Matters

Cunningham, P. (2000) 'Bilingual children: whole-school policy and practice' in M. Datta (ed.) (2000) *Bilinguality and Literacy: Principles and Practice*. London and New York: Continuum

Datta, M. (ed.) (2000) *Bilinguality and Literacy: Principles and Practice*. London and New York: Continuum

Deuchar, M. and Quay, S. (2000) *Bilingual Acquisition: Theoretical Implications of a Case Study*. Oxford: Oxford University Press

Dodwell, E. (1999) '"I can tell lots of Punjabi": developing language, and literacy with bilingual children' in J. Marsh and E. Hallett (eds) *Desirable Literacies: Approaches to Language and Literacy in the Early Years*. Thousand Oaks, CA, London and New Delhi: Sage Publications

Figueroa, R. A. (2002) 'Towards a new model of assessment' in A. J. Artiles and A. A. Ortiz (eds) *English Language Learners with Special Educational Needs*. Washington, DC and McHenry, IL: Center for Applied Linguistics and Delta Systems

Frederickson, N. and Cline, T. (2002) *Special Educational Needs, Inclusion and Diversity: A Textbook*. London: University College London

Gardner, H. (1993) *Frames of Mind*. New York: Basic Books

Genesee, F. (2001) 'Bilingual first language acquisition: exploring the limits of the language faculty', *Annual Review of Applied Linguistics* 21: 153–68

Genesee, F. (2003) 'Rethinking bilingual acquisition' in V. Cook (ed.) *Portraits of the L2 User*. Clevedon: Multilingual Matters

Genesee, F., Boivin, I. and Nicoladis, E. (1996) 'Talking with strangers: a study of bilingual children's communicative competence', *Applied Psycholinguistics* 17(4): 427–42

Gregory, E., Long, S. and Volk, D. (eds) (2004) *Many Pathways to Literacy: Young Children Learning with Siblings, Grandparents, Peers and Communities*. London and New York: RoutledgeFalmer

Grosjean, F. (1982) *Life with Two Languages: An Introduction to Bilingualism*. London: Harvard University Press

Gumperz, J. J. (1982) 'Conversational code-switching' in *Discourse Strategies*. Cambridge: Cambridge University Press

Hall, S. (1992) 'What is this "black" in popular culture?' in G. Dent (ed.) *Black Popular Culture*. Seattle: Bay Press

Hester, H. (1990) 'Stages of English learning' in M. Barrs *et al. Patterns of Learning: The Primary Language Record*. London: CLPE

Hoffman, Eva (1989) *Lost in Translation: A Life in a New Language*. New York: Dutton

Jalava, A. (1988) 'Nobody could see that I was a Finn' in T. Skuttnab-Kangas and J. Cummins (eds) (1988) *Minority Education: From Shame to Struggle*. Clevedon: Multilingual Matters

Kenner, C. (2000) 'Symbols make text: a social semiotic analysis of writing in a multilingual nursery', *Written Language and Literacy* 3(2): 235–66

Kenner, C. (2004a) 'Community school pupils reinterpret their knowledge of Chinese and Arabic for primary school peers' in E. Gregory, S. Long and D. Volk (eds) (2004) *Many Pathways to Literacy: Young Children Learning with Siblings, Grandparents, Peers and Communities*. London and New York: RoutledgeFalmer

Kenner, C. (2004b) *Becoming Biliterate: Young Children Learning Different Writing Systems*. Stoke on Trent: Trentham Books

Kenner, C. and Kress, G. (2003) 'The multisemiotic resources of biliterate children', *Journal of Early Childhood Literacy* 3(2): 179–202

Kenner, C., Kress, G., Al-Khatib, H., Kam, R. and Tsai, K.-C. (2004) 'Finding the keys to biliteracy: how young children interpret different writing systems', *Language and Education* 18(2): 124–44

Kramsch, C. (ed.) (2002) *Language Acquisition and Language Socialization: Ecological Perspectives*. London and New York: Continuum

Labov, W. (1970) 'The language of non-standard English' in F. Williams (ed.) *Language and Poverty*. Chicago: Markham

Li Wei (1994) *Three Generations: Two Languages, One Family*. Clevedon: Multilingual Matters

Li Wei (2000) 'Extending schools: bilingual development of Chinese children in Britain' in M. Datta (ed.) (2000) *Bilinguality and Literacy: Principles and Practice*. London and New York: Continuum

Long, S. with Bell, D. and Brown, J. (2004) 'Making a place for peer interaction: Mexican American kindergarteners learning language and literacy' in E. Gregory, S. Long and D. Volk (eds) (2004) *Many Pathways to Literacy: Young Children Learning with Siblings, Grandparents, Peers and Communities*. London and New York: RoutledgeFalmer

MacIntyre, P. D., Baker, S. C., Clement, R. and Nconrod, S. (2001) 'Willingness to communicate, social support, and language learning orientations of immersion students', *Studies in Second Language Acquisition* 23: 369–88

Marsh, J. and Millard, E. (2000) *Literacy and Popular Culture: Using Children's Culture in the Classroom*. London: PCP

Meadows, S. (1993) *The Child as Thinker: The Development and Acquisition of Cognition in Childhood*. London and New York: Routledge

Mehler, J., Juscyzk, P., Lambertz, G., Halsted, N., Bertoncini, J. and Amiel-Tison, C. (1988) 'A precursor of language acquisition in young infants', *Cognition* 29: 143–78

139

Meisel, J. M. (2004) 'The bilingual child', in T. K. L. Bhatia and S. W. Ritchie (eds) *The Handbook of Bilingualism*. Malden, MA: Blackwell

Mills, Jean (2001) 'Being bilingual: perspectives of third generation Asian children on language, culture and identity', *International Journal of Bilingual Education and Bilingualism* 4(6): 383–402

Mor-Sommerfield, A. (2002) 'Language mosaic: developing literacy in a second-new-language – a new perspective', *Reading, Literacy and Language* 36(3): 99–105

Murshad, A. (2002) 'Tools for talking', *Reading, Literacy and Language* 36(3): 106–12

National Conference on Heritage Languages in America (*c.* 2001) *Heritage Languages in America*. McHenry, IL: Center for Applied Linguistics

Ng, A. K. T. (1982) 'My people: the Chinese community in the north-east', *Multicultural Teaching* 4: 30–3

Pahl, K. (1999) *Transformation: Meaning Making in Nursery Education*. Stoke on Trent: Trentham Books

Painter, C. (1999) *Learning Through Language in Early Childhood*. London and New York: Cassell

Pinker, S. (1994) *The Language Instinct*. Harmondsworth: Penguin

Prout, J. (2005) *The Future of Childhood*. Abingdon and New York: Routledge-Falmer

Rampton, B. (1995) *Crossing: Language and Ethnicity amongst Adolescents*. London: Longman

Reid, S. (1993) *Lament for a Nation: The Life and Death of Canada's Bilingual Dream*. Vancouver: Arsenal Pulp Press

Rinaldi, C. (2006) *In Dialogue with Reggio Emilia: Listening, researching and learning*. London and New York: Routledge

Rogoff, B. (1990) *Apprenticeship in Thinking: Cognitive Development in Social Context*. Oxford: Oxford University Press

Rogoff, B. (2003) *The Cultural Nature of Development*. Oxford: Oxford University Press.

Rogoff, B. *et al.* (1993) 'Guided participation in cultural activities by toddlers and caregivers', Monogram Social Research, *Child Development* 58(7), ser. no. 236

Ross, M. (2000) 'Bilinguality and making learning possible in the early years' in M. Datta (ed.) (2000) *Bilinguality and Literacy: Principles and Practice*. London and New York: Continuum

Skuttnab-Kangas, T. and Cummins, J. (eds) (1988) *Minority Education: From Shame to Struggle*. Clevedon: Multilingual Matters

Smidt, S. (ed.) (1998) *The Early Years: a Reader*. London: Routledge

Smidt. S. (2006) *The Developing Child in the 21st Century: a Global Perspective on Child Development*. London and New York: Routledge

Sneddon, Raymonde (2000) 'Language and literacy: children's experiences in multilingual environments', *International Journal of Bilingual Education and Bilingualism* 4(3): 265–82

Tizard, B. and Hughes, M. (1984) *Young Children Learning: Talking and Thinking at Home and at School*. London: Fontana

UNESCO (1953) *The Use of Vernacular Languages in Education*. Paris: UNESCO

Voss, B. (1998) 'Supporting young children' in S. Smidt (ed.) (1998) *The Early Years: a Reader*. London: Routledge

Vygotsky, L. S. (1986 [1962]) *Thought and Language*. Cambridge, MA: MIT Press

Wells, G. (1986) *The Meaning Makers: Children Learning Language and Using Language to Learn*. Portsmouth: Heinemann

Williams, A. (2004) 'Playing school in multiethnic London' in E. Gregory, S. Long and D. Volk (eds) (2004) *Many Pathways to Literacy: Young Children Learning with Siblings, Grandparents, Peers and Communities*. London and New York: RoutledgeFalmer

Index